ANTHROPOLOGICAL PAPERS

MUSEUM OF ANTHROPOLOGY, UNIVERSITY OF MICHIGAN

NO. 68

THE BIOLOGICAL AND SOCIAL ANALYSES OF A MISSISSIPPIAN CEMETERY FROM SOUTHEAST MISSOURI: THE TURNER SITE, 23BU21A

BY THOMAS K. BLACK III

ANN ARBOR, MICHIGAN

1979

ISBN 978-0-932206-81-7 (paper)

ISBN 978-1-951519-03-2 (ebook)

CONTENTS

FIGURES

TABLES

PLATES

ACKNOWLEDGMENTS

This report on a small Mississippian village, the Turner site, in southeast Missouri is one of several resulting from the Powers Phase Project of the Museum of Anthropology of the University of Michigan with primary support from the National Science Foundation to James B. Griffin as Principal Investigator and James E. Price as Field Director. The primary funding was provided by the National Science Foundation Anthropology section in 1968, 1970 and 1973 under Grants GS1966, and GS3215. In addition the project was aided by grants from the undergraduate participation program of the National Science Foundation and by the University of Michigan. My own research was supported by a National Science Foundation Graduate Fellowship. A brief history of the Powers Phase Project has recently been published along with a study of the Snodgrass site by Price and Griffin [1979]. The Turner site is within a furlong of the Snodgrass site and both are part of the remains of a relatively short-lived Mississippian occupation of about A.D. 1300.

Figures 2, 3, and 4 appear through the courtesy of James E. Price. Figure 7 was redrawn by the author from the original burial map of the Turner site made by James J. Krakker. All other redrawn figures or remade tables are cited in the text.

I would like to thank my committee, Christopher S. Peebles, James B. Griffin, and C. Loring Brace, all of the University of Michigan, for their advice and criticisms of this paper which was submitted to this committee in 1976 as a Preliminary Paper. Only minor revisions and additions have been made in this published version. My good friends Jerry Voss and Jim Krakker must also be thanked for their encouragement and suggestions. In addition, I greatly appreciate the often thankless efforts of my wife, Deborah, to make this study intelligible.

Introduction

This study endeavors to show that, even under adverse circumstances, mortuary analysis can make valuable contributions to our understanding of prehistoric societies. Other authors have amply demonstrated the benefits to be gained from the detailed analysis of the burial practices of prehistoric societies. Few, however, would have suspected that a looted cemetery containing poorly preserved bone could provide much worthwhile knowledge. Yet, the analysis of the poorly preserved burials from the disturbed Turner site cemetery yields information regarding the health, stature, demography, and social organization of Turner's erstwhile inhabitants.

The examination of the Turner cemetery also represents the synthesis of physical and social analyses of prehistoric burials. This is not the first time that the biological and social analyses of a cemetery have been performed by the same individual (e.g. Buikstra 1972, Green, Green and Armelagos 1974, Lane and Sublett 1972, Spence 1974), but it is part of a trend which should become the rule in mortuary analysis. When the mortuary analyst is also the physical anthropologist, he is better able to control the sources of error from the biological analysis. The quality of the study should be further enhanced by the removal of the possibility of poor communication between the physical anthropologist and the mortuary analyst. In the special case of disturbed, poorly preserved burials, it is advisable that a single individual perform or supervise both the excavation and the analysis of the burials, since there can be many unanticipated sources of confusion.

Because this study deals with just one class of data (mortuary) taken primarily from a single site (Turner) which was only one part of the larger Powers phase society, it will raise more questions than it answers. These questions will aid in the design of future research in the Powers phase and in mortuary analysis.

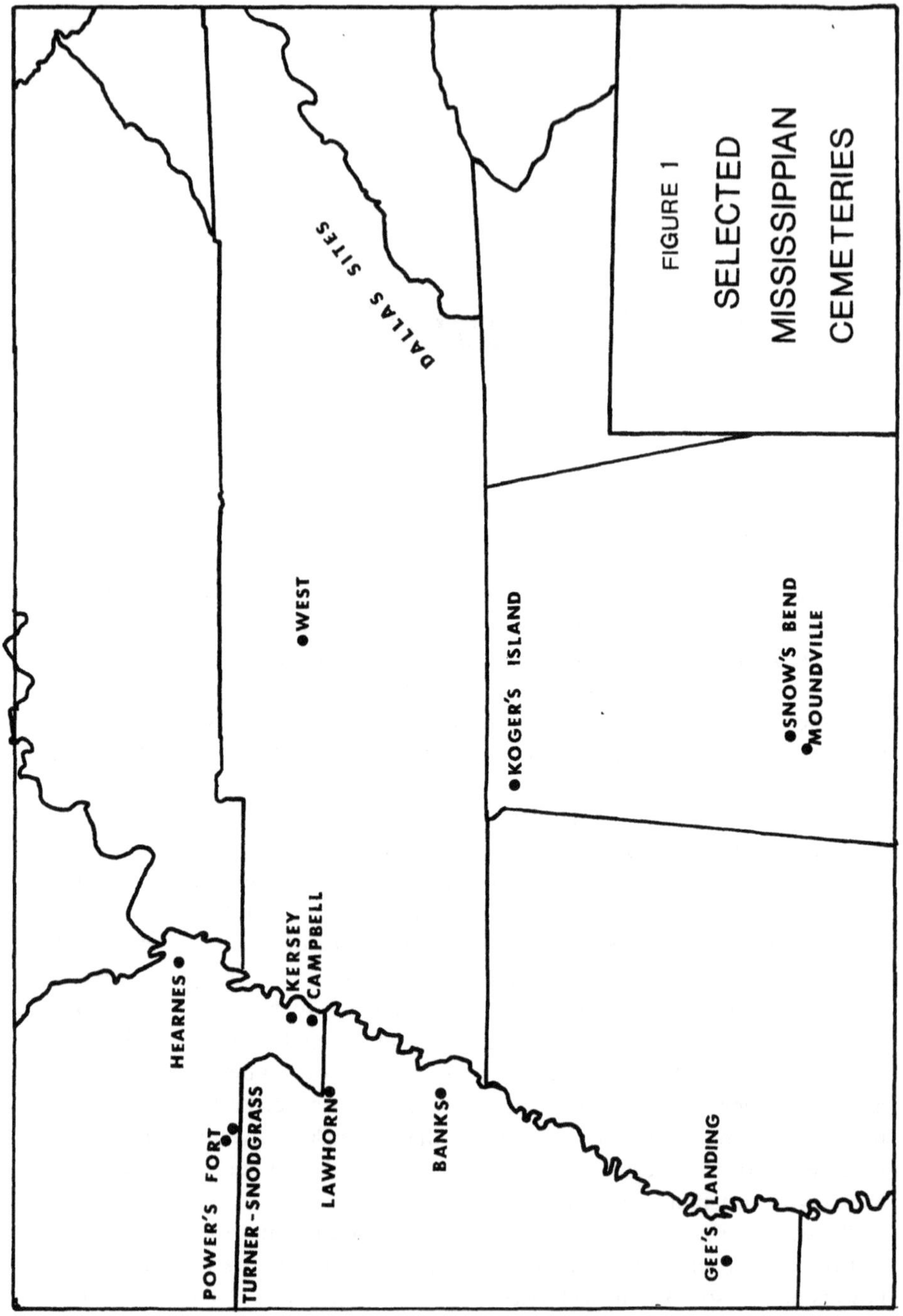

Figure 1. Selected Mississippian Cemeteries

1

Middle Mississippian Cemeteries

A Brief History of Mortuary Analysis

In 1964, Binford published his analysis of the Galley Pond Mound burials. Although the analysis itself may be disputed on several points, it heralded the reawakening of archaeological interest in the social dimensions of mortuary practices. Binford (1971) and Saxe (1970) followed by testing a number of propositions about mortuary behavior against ethnographic data. These studies provided the foundations for subsequent archaeological analyses of status and social organization as they are reflected in prehistoric burial practices (Brown 1971; Hatch 1974; Hatch and Willey 1974; Peebles 1971, 1974; Saxe 1971; Tainter 1975).

Several of these analyses investigated the social organization of Middle Mississippian societies. The term "Middle Mississippian" refers to the agricultural-based populations of the Central Mississippi Valley, between St. Louis and Vicksburg, in the period from A.D. 700 until European contact. Sites and phases of the Middle Mississippian are characterized by their dependence on an agricultural economy based on maize, beans and squash (Griffin 1967). Other traits shared by some Middle Mississippian phases include shell-tempered pottery, fortified villages with an open central plaza, substructure mounds, and a characteristic religious symbolism.

Among the analyses of the social organization of Middle Mississippian societies are Hatch and Willey's (1974) analysis of status in the Dallas society of eastern Tennessee and Peebles's (1971, 1974) analysis of Moundville and related subsidiary sites. These efforts may be contrasted with the incomplete analyses performed for the majority of excavated Middle Mississippian cemeteries.

At present, to my knowledge, no Mississippian cemetery from southeast Missouri, northeast Arkansas, or the vicinity has been subjected to a rigorous analysis for evidence of social organization. In fact, for a variety of reasons, many site reports lack even a simple analysis of individual age and sex for the cemetery population. The state of mortuary analysis in the region of southeast Missouri is documented below. The examples discussed here were found by an examination of several of the archaeological and anthropological journals published in Arkansas, Missouri, and Tennessee (Fig. 1).

The best reported Mississippian cemeteries in the region were from the Campbell site in Pemiscot County, Missouri (Chapman and Anderson 1955; Spier 1955). Virtually all the information needed for a detailed mortuary analysis was provided in the reports, although this was before mortuary analysis had become a recognized subject for investigation. The data provided within the reports include age, sex, and stature for each individual, the burial accompaniments and their placement, burial orientation, and a map showing the relationships of the burials to each other. The site and the cemeteries were not completely excavated, so it is difficult to be certain that the sample excavated is representative of all burials at the site.

Another Pemiscot County site, the Kersey site, was reported by Marshall in 1965. Some of the necessary information for a social analysis is provided, but no analysis was attempted. This may have been because two Mississippian phases were present at the site, and it was difficult to separate them.

At the Hearnes site, Mississippi County, Missouri, the archaeologists were frustrated by extremely poor bone preservation which prevented any osteological analysis (Klippel 1969).

Preservation was again a complicating factor at the Lawhorn site in Mississippi County, Arkansas (Nash 1962). The information contained in the report is inadequate for further analyses.

The burials at the Banks site in Crittenden County, Arkansas, were extremely well-preserved (Perino 1966). Unfortunately, Perino chose to describe only a few "unusual" burials out of the hundreds of burials which were excavated at Banks. Because the information on the burials provided in the site report is biased, it should not be used for any physical or social analysis.

The Gee's Landing cemetery in Drew County, Arkansas, was excavated by amateurs who were interested in collecting pots but who also wanted to report their activities (White 1970). They did not bother to save any human bones other than one skull, so no physical analysis could be made.

The West site in Davidson County, Tennessee, was excavated and reported by amateurs (Dowd 1972). They submitted some of the osteological material to physical anthropologists for analysis (Wright, Stone, and Bass 1973). Unfortunately, the data presented in the two reports are insufficient for analysis.

Seven sites have been mentioned in this brief survey. At two of them, bone preservation was so poor that it interfered with analysis. At another site, the complicated archaeological situation made analysis difficult. Three sites were ideal for analysis, but the necessary data were not collected. Only the Campbell site, which was excavated over 20 years ago, was reported in sufficient detail for analysis.

The Powers Phase

The Powers phase was a Middle Mississippian society of southeast Missouri (Fig. 2). The largest site of the phase is Powers Fort, 23BU10, which is located on the edge of the Ozark escarpment in Butler County. It is the only site with any mounds, four in all, and it may have served as the ceremonial center of the phase. At least ten villages of 1.5 to 3 acres are located within seven miles of Powers Fort in the lowlands to the south and east. These villages include from 40-100 structures each. The burials from two of these villages, Turner and Snodgrass, are described and analyzed in this report. There are also in the region a number of smaller sites containing two to ten structures. These sites are referred to as hamlets. In addition, there are many small, scattered, limited activity sites such as hunting camps.

The archaeological affinities of the Powers phase are to the south and east in the St. Francis area of northeast Arkansas and the Cairo Lowland of southeast Missouri. The Powers phase "is not indigenous to the Little Black River area but came in fully developed bringing with it a cultural pattern which emerged further east and south in the Mississippi River Delta" (Price 1973:16). The Powers phase is thought to have existed no more than 50 to 100 years around A.D. 1300 in the Little Black River area. Although Powers Fort may have been inhabited most of this time, the Snodgrass site (and presumably, the Turner site) probably was occupied no more than two years (Price 1973).

The physiographic setting of the Powers phase sites is characterized by alluvial deposits formed by the braided channels of the ancient Mississippi River sometime before 8000 B.C. Present day streams in the area follow the main channels of the ancient Mississippi, since these channels are lower than the surrounding ancient floodplain. These modern streams have formed their own floodplains at a lower elevation than the old Mississippi River, and so do not flood the higher deposits left by that river. These ancient deposits take the form of sand ridges rising 15 to 20 ft. above the general 300 ft. elevation of the region. The sand ridges had soil which was easily tilled by aboriginal techniques, were dry throughout the year, and were preferred locations for the Powers phase agriculturalists. The Turner, 23BU21A, and Snodgrass, 23BU21B, sites occupy Sharecropper Ridge, separated about 200 yd. from each other by a swale which was probably inundated seasonally.

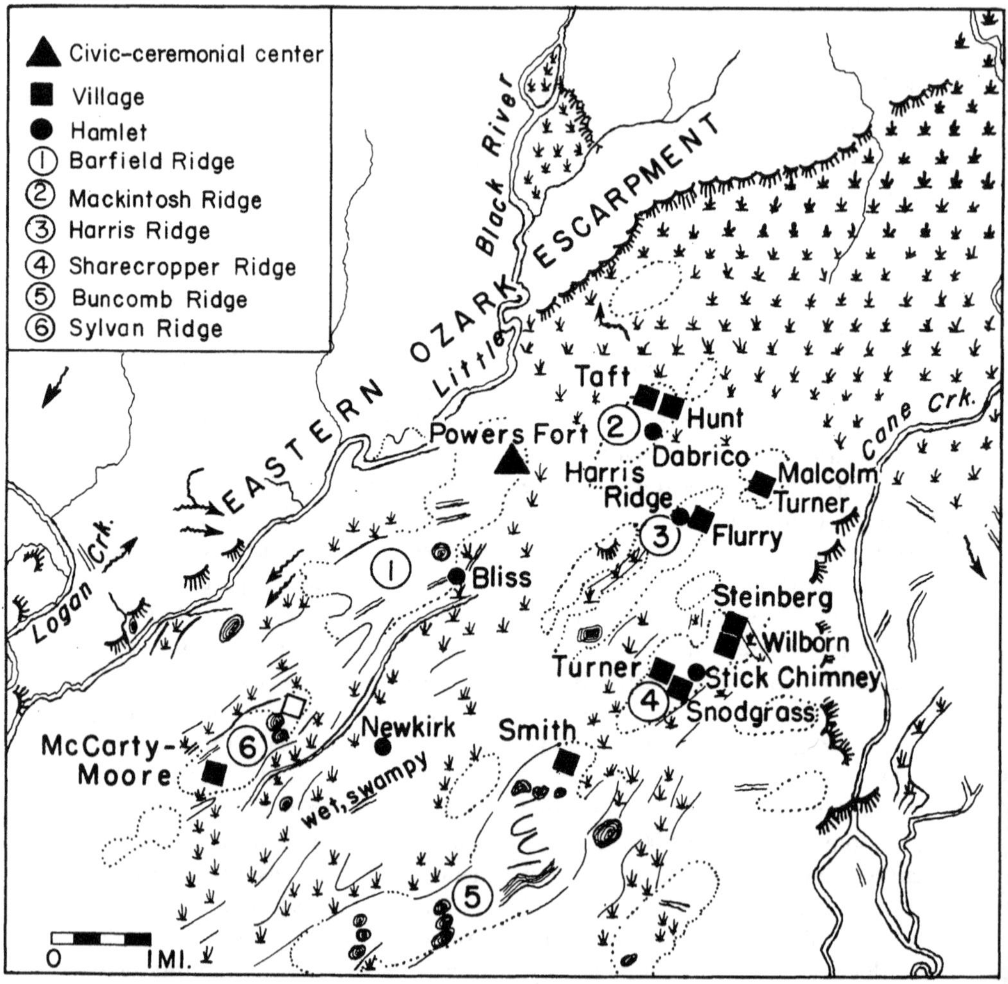

Figure 2. Powers Phase Settlement System

The Powers Phase Burials

Excavations of Powers phase sites have been conducted since 1964. During the course of these excavations, human skeletal remains have been recovered from three sites: Powers Fort, Turner, and Snodgrass (Price and Griffin 1979).

Five adult burials from widely separated areas were excavated at Powers Fort in 1964, 1965, and 1969. In addition, three infant burials were found in 1969 under the floor of the only structure excavated at Powers Fort. The adult burials were excavated because they had been exposed by agricultural activity and were in danger of imminent destruction. Because of the very limited nature of these excavations, it could not be determined whether a cemetery or several cemeteries were present at Powers Fort.

Excavations were carried out at the Snodgrass site (Fig. 3) from 1968 through 1973, during which time the village was nearly completely excavated (Price 1973). Six adult burials were found in the village, but there was no cemetery. A number of infants were buried beneath structure floors at Snodgrass.

The Turner site (Fig. 4) was excavated from 1966 to 1968, and again in 1972 and 1973. Like Snodgrass, there is little chance that any structure was missed at Turner. Only one infant was recovered from beneath the structure floors at Turner, although others may have been missed. Unlike Snodgrass, Turner had a large cemetery in the center of the site. The cemetery was completely excavated, revealing a total of 54 burials containing a minimum of 118 individuals. Most of the burials in the Turner cemetery were arranged in five rows which were aligned along a north-northeast to south-southwest axis (Fig. 7). The burials themselves are oriented perpendicularly to the axes of the rows. A few burials could represent additional "rows" which contained only one burial each.

Problems with the Powers Phase Burials

In general, the skeletal material from Powers Fort was in a very good state of preservation, that from Snodgrass was fair, and that from Turner was poor to fair (Pl. 1-5). The situation at Turner was further aggravated by four major factors. First, some of the burials were damaged by agricultural activities which brought bone to the surface. Second, the presence of human bone and of the cemetery became known to pothunters, who descended on the site in great numbers. Because of the alluvial origin of the sand ridges, no rocks occur naturally in them. This makes the use of a metal probe a very effective means for detecting buried solid objects, such as pots. By employing these probes, pothunters managed to discover and remove at least 70 percent of the pottery in the cemetery. Only 13 pots were found by archaeologists,

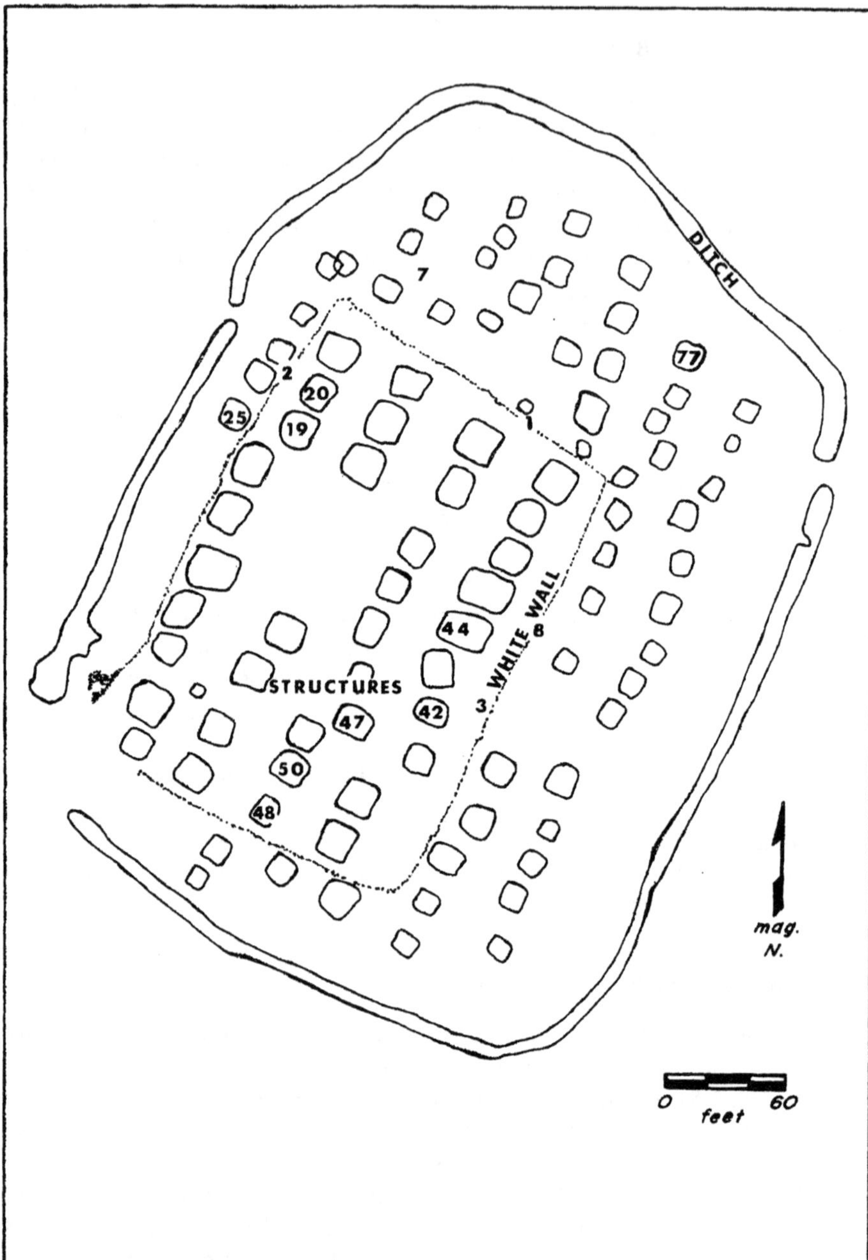

Figure 3. Snodgrass Site

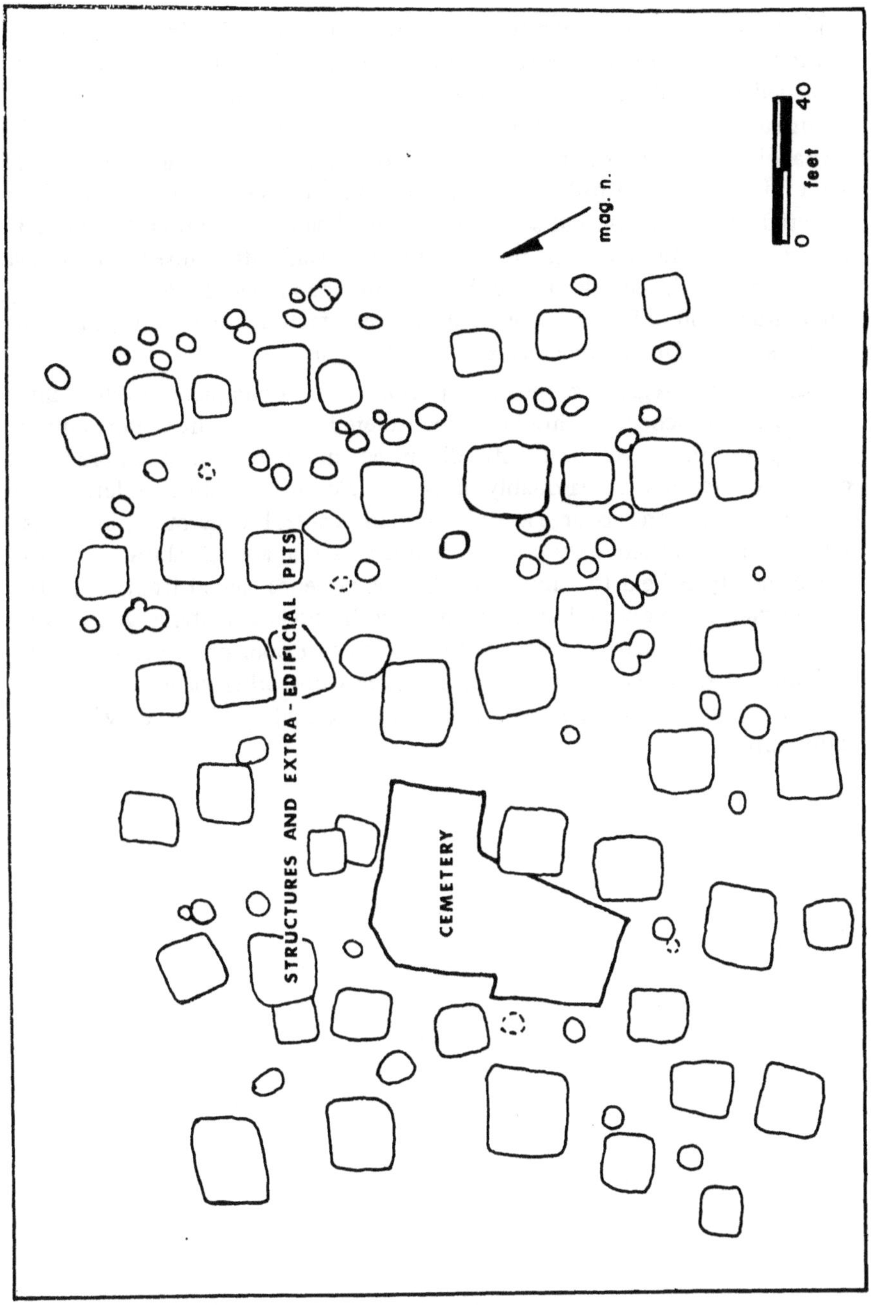

Figure 4. Location of the Cemetery on the Turner Site

while pothunters are known to have recovered at least 29. In the process of unearthing the pots, the looters disturbed at least 30 burials and extensively damaged many of them (Pl. 3). The third aggravating factor was the lack of adequate care in the excavation and recording of the disturbed burials by the archaeologists. For example, there are no notes accompanying the maps of some of the badly disturbed burials. The fourth difficulty is that some of the material has been lost and some intermingled since excavation, but prior to the commencement of the present study. Several other investigators have done some work with the Turner burials, but abandoned the project at a very early stage and left few notes. All of these factors combine to make the analysis of the Turner cemetery a formidable task.

Rather than regarding the Turner cemetery as a complete disaster that is best left untouched, it should be considered an excellent opportunity to develop techniques to deal with disturbed and fragmentary material. The cemetery presents a reasonably large sample of individual skeletons and burials, but not one so large as to be unmanageable. Furthermore, Turner is a single component site only briefly occupied, so that aboriginal disturbance of the cemetery is held to a minimum. The experience gained from excavating the Turner cemetery and from examining the skeletal material will make it possible to anticipate and deal with problems of poor preservation and disturbance at other Powers phase sites. At least one other village is known to have a cemetery, and another may have a cemetery, both of which are undisturbed.

2

Description of the Burials

Designation of Individuals in Burials

The task of identifying and labeling individuals and their bones within many of the burials from the Turner site has been complicated by several circumstances. First, different methods of labeling skeletons in multiple burials were used for each field season. In the first season, every individual was given a separate burial number. An example of this system is Burials 8 and 9 which were parts of a multiple burial. Later, individuals were numbered so that, for example, Burial 13 had skeleton-1, skeleton-2, etc. In 1972, individual skeletons were assigned letters so that there was a 36A and a 36B. In 1973, the individual bones were numbered or were labeled by their position within the burial as in "53 east and 53 west." It is here decided to adopt as a uniform convention the system used in 1972.

The second difficulty involves the accidental mixture of several burials or individuals. In some of the burials where individuals were designated in the field, the remains have since become intermingled making it impossible in most cases to determine which individual is which. For example, a mistake by a lab worker caused the pieces of the three crania of Burial 28 to become inseparably mixed.

A related problem resulted from the frequent use of multiple bundle burials by the Turner site inhabitants. Because of the partial disintegration of many of the bones, it is not possible to tell which femora go with which pelves or which crania go with which dentitions. It is possible to pair many of the femora together on the basis of length, robusticity, and circumference. Thus it can be said that there are at least four individuals represented by femora in Burial 52. However, it is uncertain which dentitions should go with which femora. Still it is desirable to have a means of identifying the individual represented by two femora, or by a certain calotte, or by a dozen loose teeth. In order to achieve this end, a multiple designation system for these bundle burials has been chosen. Individuals identified by dentitions will be assigned letters, as is the standard practice for multiple burials where individuals were separable. Individuals represented by femora will be identified by the letter *F* and the numbers assigned to their femur fragments, as for example F-1 and F-5 from Burial 52. Individuals who were identified by cranial fragments are labeled CF, as is the case with the occipital from Burial 54 which is designated Burial 54 CF-1. Individuals who were identified by pelvic fragments are labeled *P*, for instance B-5 P-1.

The most confusing case is the "Moore House Basement Burials." A number of burials and parts of burials, wrapped in plaster casts, were removed from the Turner site and stored in the basement of the Moore House, the Powers Phase Project headquarters. Subsequently, the combined actions of moisture, slugs, and rats destroyed the casts and mixed the bones. When the bones were salvaged from the basement and cleaned, they were quite soft and fragile, but upon drying they proved to be the best preserved bones from Turner. Unfortunately, no one remembered which burials they were from, only that they had to be among the first 20 burials because the bones were in casts. Since the field notes for Burials 10 and 11 are missing, it is even more difficult to assign the remains to particular burials. The "Basement Burials" could include: three crania from B-5; an unknown number of individuals from B-1, B-2, B-10, and B-11; two crania and some post-cranial bones from B-13; one cranium and most of two post-cranial skeletons from B-16; and one skull from B-19. The remains recovered included five dentitions, most of three calvaria, fragments of five left and seven right femora, and fragments of three left and two right tibiae, all of them from adults. Since there is no basis for assigning any of the remains to any particular burial, they have been lumped into a single group and called "Burial 61." All three methods of identification of individuals are used with these specimens: B-61A is a face with teeth; 61B through 61E are mandibles, some with associated maxillary teeth. Four separate calvaria and cranial fragments are labeled 61 CF-1 through 61 CF-4; and seven different pairings of femurs carry "F" designations, such as 61 F-1 and F-10. There is a minimum of seven individuals represented (the seven right femora were the most numerous skeletal element), but it is impossible to say which post-cranial bones are associated with which mandibles. Each individual was aged and sexed to the extent that it was possible. The sexual composition of the "Burial" was then determined as follows: three female and two indeterminate sex crania; two female and three indeterminate pelves; five female and two male sets of femora. Thus the minimum number of males is two and of females is five, which is compatible with the initial estimate of the number of individuals represented on the basis of bone count.

There are a few other cases of mixed remains. The field notes suggest that Burials 1, 3, and 4 at Turner may represent the same individual. This can not be, since the cranium in Burial 3 is from a child, while the tibiae of Burial 4 are adult. These three are considered to be separate burials. Burials 8 and 9 are actually part of one multiple burial and will be called Burial 8. The individual labeled "B-9" will be referred to as B-8D in this report. Burial 42, excavated in 1973, was discovered upon completion of the cemetery map to be part of B-6, excavated in 1966. Since the remains of B-11 were mixed in with those of B-6, the three Burials 6, 11, and 42 will be considered together except for the few instances when individual bones can be identified. The designation "B-42" will be abandoned and "B-6" will be understood to include those remains excavated as B-42. Burial 17 lacked a post-cranial skeleton, but is close enough to B-38 that it may well be part of the multiple burial. This also helps to account for the extra temporal from B-17. This and other evidence is sufficient, and the designation "B-17" is dropped in favor of "B-38." Completion of the cemetery map also showed Burials 31 and 50 to be part of the same multiple burial. The designation "B-50" is abandoned, and the fragments are reassigned to the proper individuals in B-31. Burial 58 is a pothole with a few bones tossed in; it is not a true burial. The remains of this individual or individuals will not be considered as a separate burial for the purposes of the burial-by-burial minimum counts in Appendix C. Burial 54, a collection of cranial fragments from at least three individuals, may also represent the work of pothunters. Once again, the remains are not considered as part of a burial in Appendix C. Burials 54 and 58 are included in the cemetery inventory done on a bone-by-bone basis (Appendix D). Neither B-54 nor B-58 is considered in the investigation of the Turner site mortuary practices. Thus, although 60 burials were designated at Turner, there were only 54 present. Field notes have been lost for two burials, 10 and 11, and are inadequate for some of the burials excavated during the early years of the Powers Phase Project. The skeletal material from B-39 never reached the lab and could not be accounted for. To further complicate matters, some of the material from Turner was worked over by several individuals before the present inquiry was begun. Some of the material was mixed together, some was misidentified, and probably, some was lost. These difficulties pertain only to the first 20 burials. The problems with each burial will be dealt with during the discussion of the burials which follows.

Two methods of identifying burials to indicate locations were used at Turner. Almost all of the burials came from the cemetery and were assigned numbers (Fig. 7). In addition, a few infant burials were found beneath structure floors. These sub-floor burials were assigned the number of the structure under which they were found; for example, STR 27 B-1.

At Snodgrass, there was no cemetery as such, but several burials were found at locations scattered across the site, both outside of and underneath structures (Fig. 3). Several burials from beneath structures were assigned numbers from the general series (without the prefix "STR X"), while one burial from outside a structure was assigned a structure number in combination with its general series number. The remains of eight sub-floor burials were examined in the lab. Seven were infants and one was adult. Another individual was recognized when Bruce Smith found human bone fragments among the burned animal bone excavated from Structure 19. Two burials from the general series (numbers 5 and 6) were identified on the burial forms as infants, but they were never located in the lab. Burials 5 and 6 should have been labeled "STR 19 B-1" and "STR 20 B-1." Burial 4 was found under Structure 25 and should have been called "STR 25 B-1." The other general series burials, Burials 1, 2, 3, 7 and 8, were properly identified.

The burials at Powers Fort were assigned numbers according to the same system that was used at Turner. One burial contained two individuals which were originally designated B-3 and B-4. For the purposes of this report, they are renumbered B-3A and B-3B, respectively.

All of the burials analyzed in this report are described in the following pages.

Sex Determination

Three methods of sex assessment were used on the Powers phase burials in an attempt to determine the sex of as many individuals as possible. The methods of sexing were based on the observation of the pelvis, the cranium, and the femur. Most of the other skeletal elements were so fragmentary as to preclude their use for the determination of sex. The use of three approaches permitted the cross-validation of the different methods.

The most reliable method of sexing was based on the examination of the pelvis. Because of poor preservation, not one pubic symphysis was recovered. Thus it was impossible to use the Phenice technique of sexing which has been shown to be accurate to a percentage of 95+ (Phenice 1969a). However, the sciatic notch and sometimes the pre-auricular sulcus could be examined for 53 adult innominates, of which 35 were complete enough to sex. There was a wide range in the expression of the two traits, but little difficulty was experienced in assigning sexes to the innominates. This method resulted in the determination of 10 males, 19 females, and 24 individuals of indeterminate sex (including six of the individuals with complete sciatic notches). The results of this method of sex determination are presented in Table 62 in Appendix B.

Sexing by the sciatic notch is probably 80 to 90 percent accurate. Washburn

(1948) stated that "the sex of over 75% of pelves can be determined by the (sciatic) notch alone." In 1949, he tested this with 152 Bantu and 55 Bushman skeletons. If the average of the mean male and female widths of the sciatic notches is used as a dividing point for assigning sex to the individuals in these two samples, an accuracy of about 87 percent is achieved.

The second method of sexing involved the examination of the restored crania for traits useful for sexual diagnosis. The characteristics which proved most useful for distinguishing sex were: a) mastoid size, b) presence or absence of external occipital protuberance, c) development of nuchal ridges, d) presence and size of the supraorbital ridges, e) roundness of orbital margins, f) size and robusticity of the mandible, g) size and robusticity of the zygomatic processes, h) form of the frontal, and i) skull size. There were 53 adult crania sufficiently well-preserved for these criteria to be employed. Of these, 23 were male, 19 female, and 11 indeterminate (Table 63, App. B).

The assessments of sex based on cranial form are probably no more than 80 to 90 percent accurate. Stewart (1948) claimed to be no more than 80 percent accurate using the skull alone, and said that Hrdlicka was about 90 percent accurate using the skull and mandible.

Although the crania were sexed independently of the pelves, there were no contradictory results in any of the cases where association between cranial and post-cranial remains could be definitely established. Had there been a contradiction, the individual in question would first have been checked to make certain of the association between the skull and the pelvis. If this failed to resolve the difficulty, the pelvic sex would be assigned to the individual. Sex as determined from the pelvis was compatible with sex as determined from the cranium for 16 individuals (13A, 13B, 15, 21A, 25A, 33A, 33B, 34, 35B, 36A, and 36B from Turner; 7 from Snodgrass; and 1 and 2 from Powers Fort).

The third method of sexing was based on the circumference of the femur. During the examination of the burials, it becamse apparent that the adult femora were quite variable not only in length, but in robusticity and circumference. When the lengths of bone segments were measured for the estimation of stature, the femur circumference at midshaft also was measured with a cloth tape. The average measurement error was 0.5 mm. After the cranial and pelvic sexes of the population had been determined, the femur circumference was analyzed for the 17 females and 9 males for whom sex was most certain and the association of the femur with the pelvis or skull was definite. In cases where both of an individual's femora were available, their midshaft circumferences were averaged. There was no overlap between the female range (68 to 82 mm) and the male range (88.5 to 97.2 mm). The mean and standard deviation were calculated for each sex (male: mean=92.3, s.d.=3.56; female:

mean=75.3, s.d.=4.42). A *t*-test for two populations with unknown and unequal variance was performed. Using the sample sizes and variances, the degrees of freedom was calculated to be 21. The calculated value for the t-statistic was 10.62, which greatly exceeded the test value ($t_{.005,21}$) of 2.831. It would appear that the two samples were not drawn from the same population.

Assuming that both samples were from normal distributions, cut-off points for 95 percent confidence intervals for each mean were calculated. The female confidence intervals for each mean were calculated. The female confidence interval was 66.5 to 84.2 mm, while the male interval was 85.5 to 98.9 mm. Using these figures as a guideline, sexes were assigned to the femora as follows: midshaft circumference less than 84.2 mm was female; circumference from 84.2 to 85.5 mm was indeterminate; circumference greater than 85.5 mm was male. This made it possible to sex still more individuals and provided only one contradictory result–individual 13C of the Turner site. This person had a female skull and male femora. However, the association between the skull and the femor is far from certain, since a double bundle burial rested on the legs of 13 C, and her legs may have been misidentified in the field.

Following the guidelines from the Turner population, 24 femora were assigned male sex and 56 were assigned female sex (Table 64, App. B). For the combined Powers phase sample, a total of 27 males and 60 females was identified by femur circumference. It is difficult to explain this extreme imbalance. If the difference between the mean circumference of the male and female femur samples is fortuitous, it is surprising that the difference is so large and so significant.

The method does not seem to be at fault. A variant of the method has been tested with a sample of 63 males and 51 females from the prehistoric Libben site in northeastern Ohio. These burials had been sexed with 99 percent accuracy (C. Owen Lovejoy: personal communication). The femoral circumference method sexed 85 percent of these individuals correctly (Black 1978a). It is assumed that the Powers phase material was sexed by this method with equal accuracy and that the male/female imbalance is real.

Age Determination

The juveniles of the Powers phase were aged by the calcification of their mandibular teeth (Moorrees, Fanning, and Hunt 1963). In the few cases where maxillary teeth were available but mandibular teeth were lacking, age was based on the state of eruption of the maxillary teeth (Brothwell 1965) (Table 60, App. A). A few juvenile burials were toothless and could not be aged by dental development. One of these was aged by the development of the occipital bone (Redfield 1970). These ages could not be checked against post-cranial indicators of age, such as the appearance and fusion of the epiphyses, because the post-cranial bones of the children were extremely fragmentary.

Infants of the Powers phase were aged by the development of the occipital bone (Redfield 1970) (Table 59, App. A).

Two methods were tried in an attempt to age the adult Powers phase burials. The first, osteonal remodeling, did not give results commensurate with the time and effort invested in it. The second, dental attrition, was a more successful means of determining age.

The osteonal remodeling technique of aging was first described by Kerley (1965, 1969, 1970), but has since been refined by other authors (Ahlqvist and Damsten 1969; Singh and Gunberg 1970). It is a quantitative histological procedure based on the lifelong process of remodeling of the cortical bone. As age increases, so do the numbers of osteons and osteon fragments. The cross-sectional density of osteons and osteon fragments is computed for each individual at a standardized location that is presumed to be free of exceptional stress or muscle pull. This measure may then be fitted to regression equations derived from samples of known age, and an age may be assigned to the specimen.

The advantage of this technique is that it should be free of individual bias in aging, unlike the techniques based on assessments of gross morphological changes of the pubis or closure of the cranial sutures. Furthermore, the most useful of the traditional age indicators are frequently missing or damaged (not one pubic symphysis has yet been recovered from a Powers phase site). All of the researchers mentioned above used the midshaft of the femur as one of their sites for cross-sectioning. The femur is the post-cranial bone most often preserved in good condition, and thus is more often available for aging than the pelvis (Ubelaker 1974).

Despite the fact that the rate of remodeling may be related to race and to physical activity, Ubelaker has had reasonable success using regression equations based on Caucasoid samples to age prehistoric Indian bones (Ubelaker 1974). He found somewhat different mortality patterns for his samples aged by osteonal remodeling than he found for those aged by changes of the pubic symphysis. The sample sizes were different, and it was not possible to associate femora with their pelves, so he was unable to determine if the white regression equations were really appropriate for a prehistoric Indian population.

The Powers phase skeletal material seemed ideally suited to be a test of the usefulness of osteonal remodeling as a measure for estimating age. Many of the burials were disturbed, particularly at the head. Skulls were usually broken open along the sutures, effectively eliminating suture closure as a means of aging. Besides, the technique based on suture closure has been shown to be very unreliable (Singer 1953; Brooks 1955; McKern and Stewart 1957). More adults in the Turner cemetery were represented by femora than by any other bone fragment (76 by femora to 60 by the dentition), so that a larger sample population could be developed for demographic purposes. It was hoped that the successful use of the osteonal method of aging would show archaeologists that age and sex determination are possible from poorly preserved and badly disturbed osteological material, and would help convince them of the value of excavating looted cemeteries.

Because the bone was weak, it was necessary to find an embedding medium to support it. The first medium tried was a catalyzed plastic called "Crystal Coat" purchased at a local hobby store. Femur sections were hand ground until they were about 3 mm thick and were then cleaned ultrasonically and embedded. After the plastic had hardened, the sections were ground down to about 25 microns. The slides prepared from the sections were totally unsatisfactory. No details of the internal structure of the bone could be discerned with an optical microscope.

After the initial setback, the geology department was instrumental in a second attempt to use Kerley's method. Dr. Eric Assene made the facilities of the thin-section lab available at no charge for the preparation of two test specimens. Jim Hinchcliffe, the technician, embedded two femur sections in boat resin. These specimens were ground flat on one side which was glued to a slide. The sample was then machine sawed and ground to a thickness of about 50 microns. It was then sanded by hand on 600 fine sandpaper. One of the samples showed no detail under either transmitted or reflected light microscopes. The other showed some details, but they were too poorly defined to permit the necessary distinctions.

The project was temporarily abandoned until a new possibility appeared. A block of bone was sanded smooth on one side, cleaned, mounted, and examined under the scanning electron microscope. Next the specimen was photographed, thus creating a permanent record. Osteons could then be counted on the photograph rather than in the grid of a reticule inserted in a microscope. Sections of bone were removed from the midshafts of femora from Burials 20, 33A, and 36B, all from Turner. Although all of the 12 specimens prepared from the three bones showed the central canals of the osteons, only one showed any of the circumferential lamellae which are critical for the definite identification of osteons and for the determination of the area they occupy. Etching with acid seemed to be a reasonable solution to the difficulty, because it was expected that differential erosion of the bone would give relief to the features of interest. Two concentrations of acetic acid, of

10 and 20 percent solutions, were tried for varying lengths of time without success. A new set of microphotographs showed no improvement over the first series on the same specimens.

After the failure of the osteonal remodeling technique of aging, the only reasonably accurate method remaining which could be used on a fairly large number of adults was dental attrition. This method is subject to a number of difficulties. There can be a great deal of individual variation in the wear of the teeth. This may be dependent on the hardness of the enamel, the amount of grit in the diet, the use of the teeth as tools, the loss of other teeth, bruxism, malocclusion, and other factors. Notwithstanding these concerns, dental attrition can often provide a fairly good estimate of an individual's age if the technique is used within a population.

Miles (1963) was satisfied with the results he obtained when he used dental attrition to age a British Anglo-Saxon population. He used as a baseline the teeth of children aged by dental eruption (the Powers phase children were aged by dental calcification). The functional ages of other teeth were determined by the amount of wear they showed when compared to the children's teeth. The series was built up as follows. An individual known to be ten years old by the stage of eruption of his canines and premolars was said to have first molars with a functional age of four years, since the first molars usually erupt at age six. Similarly, an adult with a third molar showing a functional age of four years would then be assumed to be 22 years old, because the third molar erupts at about age 18. His first molar would have a functional age of 16 years. Proceeding in this manner, every individual in the population who retained his molars could be aged.

The analysis of dental attrition of the Powers phase dentitions was patterned after Miles's analysis with a few modifications. Although Miles used only mandibles in his study, maxillae were included in the age determinations for the Powers phase burials. Miles's standards of attrition were not used, as there was no reason to believe that the Powers phase teeth wore at a rate similar to the Anglo-Saxon teeth. When the analysis of the Powers phase teeth was completed, it was apparent that Miles's standards of wear would have worked nearly as well as those developed for the Missouri sample (Table 1). The accuracy of the estimates is presumed to decrease with increasing age, so estimates of error are provided with the assigned ages (Table 61, App. A).

Although occlusal attrition of the tooth crowns appears heavy when contrasted with modern White populations, it is not excessive for prehistoric agriculturalists. It certainly can not be classed as heavy, and is much less severe than that seen on Australian Aborigine molars (C. Loring Brace: personal communication).

TABLE 1 Approximate Degree of Tooth Wear by Age

Age	*Tooth*	*Wear*
20	M1	A single spot of dentin may show through at the cusps.
	M2	There is some flattening of the cusps but no dentin is exposed.
	M3	The cusps are barely worn.
30	M1	The cusps are nearly flat. Multiple spots of dentin are exposed. Some grooves are obliterated.
	M2	The cusps are fairly flat but retain more relief than M1. No dentin is exposed.
	M3	The cusps are lightly worn, often with a single small flat area.
40	M1	Dentin is exposed in the form of small islands where the cusps were. The islands of dentin are not coalesced.
	M2	The tooth is worn flat with some islands of dentin exposed. The islands of dentin are smaller than M1.
	M3	The cusps are flat with spots of dentin showing through.
50	M1	The exposed surface of the tooth is nearly all dentin with an island of enamel.
	M2	Large islands of dentin are exposed.
	M3	The tooth is flat. Larger spots of dentin are exposed.
60	M1	There is essentially no enamel on the occlusal surface. Grooves are worn into the softer dentin.
	M2	Exposed dentin covers 2/3 of the crown or more.
	M3	About 1/3 to 1/2 of the occlusal surface is dentin.

The Turner Site Human Remains

BONE FOUND OUTSIDE THE CEMETERY

Structure 11. A fragment of an adult maxilla with the left canine and empty sockets for the lateral incisor and third premolar was found on the skim floor of Structure 11.

Structure 27, Burial 1 (July 1972). Fragments of an infant cranium, including the petrous part of the right temporal, were found in Pit 1 of Structure 27. Associated with the burial was a badly broken short-necked bottle with red pigment on the interior.

Structure 32, Field Specimen 62 (July 1972; 28.7S/26.0W). A seven in. fragment of the left femur of a juvenile or a female was found in a house pit. It is not clear which burial this bone belongs to, but it is nearest to B-24. A mandible fragment also found in Structure 32 belongs to B-25A; however, B-25A has both of its femora.

Extra-Edificial Pit 63 (July 1973; 10.6N/5.3E). A lightly worn upper fourth premolar was found in Extra-Edificial Pit 63.

THE CEMETERY

Burial 1 (June 1966; 25 N/11W). The excavator thought B-1 intruded on Burials 3 and 4. It is suggested in the field notes that three individuals were incompletely represented in this poorly preserved bundle burial. Only a few post-cranial bones, probably from the same adult individual, were found in the lab. No artifacts were recovered.

Burial 2 (June 1966; around 20N/10W). This disturbed burial was located near Burials 1, 3, and 4, but was not mapped. Although the field notes state that only one individual was represented, it is likely that two were present. A right femur (F-1) is probably from an adult female, but a left femur fragment (F-2) is massive enough to have come from an adult male. The cranial fragments may belong to two different individuals, but this can not be shown conclusively. The external occipital protuberance on one cranial fragment (CF1) is fairly pronounced and probably belongs to a male. A large late Archaic projectile point was found mixed in with the bones.

Burial 3 (June 1966; 20N/9W). The skull of a child aged 5.5 ±1 years was found lying on its left side facing southwest near B-1. Preservation was good, and the skull was undisturbed. No artifacts were found with the burial.

Burial 4 (June 1966; 23N/15W). An adult represented by both lower legs and one arm was located just west of Burials 1 and 3. It may have been part of an extended burial with the head to the east-southeast. The arm has been lost, but when the legs were removed from their cast, they were found to be crossed at the ankles with the right leg on top. The bones were well preserved and were described as undisturbed in the field notes, although several probe holes pass through the right tibia. B-4 was estimated to be about 163 cm tall.

Several sherds were illustrated on the field map of the burial but were not mentioned in the notes.

Burial 5 (June 1966; 28N/5W) (Pl. 1). Three extended, complete, excellently preserved adults were located on the north side of the cemetery. Their heads pointed to the east-southeast. A fourth individual, a juvenile, was not noticed in the field notes but was recognized in the lab. The juvenile was represented by a fragment of an immature innominate, the distal epiphysis of a left femur, and the unfused head of a humerus or femur. Judging from the size of the distal femur, the juvenile was probably aged between ten and 15 years. Individual A was located to the left of Individual C who was lying on her right side with her legs slightly flexed. Lying on top and between these two individuals was Individual B. A and B were completely represented in the lab, except for the crania and pelves, and were sexed by femur circumference. Individual A was a male and Individual B was a female. Individual C was unrepresented in the lab. Two female pelves (P-1 and P-2) were unlabeled; it was assumed they belonged to B (already sexed) and C (previously unsexed). Individual A's stature was estimated to be 164 cm. A large, short-necked bottle was found nearest the heads of B and C, and a large sherd was found just to the south of A. Abundant ceramic and lithic debris incorporated in the fill suggests this was one of the later burials at the Turner site. The burial was apparently undisturbed.

Burials 6, 11, and 42 (July 1966, June 1973; 4N/32W, B-6). Sometime prior to 1972, the bones of Burials 6 and 11 were mixed together in the field or in the lab. No notes accompanied the map of B-6, and the map and notes to B-11 have been lost. Because of this, only bones that had been labeled could be separated by burial. When the cemetery map was made, it was discovered that Burials 6 and 42 were, in fact, parts of the same multiple burial. For these reasons, the skeletal inventory is divided into three categories: definitely from B-6 (including B-42), definitely from B-11, and bone from either B-6 or B-11. All the bone was in poor condition.

A minimum of eight individuals was identified for the burials. Four adults of indeterminate sex and one juvenile were identified from cranial fragments. Two adults from B-11, aged about 21 (11B) and 51 (11A), were identified from mandible fragments. The other two adults were from B-6. Only one of them, B-6A, a 37-year-old with an undeformed skull, could be aged. The juvenile, B-6C, comprised a frontal, both temporals, and a tooth found with the B-42 part of B-6. B-6C is probably under age 11, since the tooth is a deciduous upper right second molar.

Seven adults, one male, five females, and one of indeterminate sex, were represented by 11 femora. One female and the male definitely came from B-6, and one female (femora 6 and 10) definitely came from B-11 (probably

Individual B). The other four individuals are of uncertain assignment. The female represented by femora 1 and 8 was estimated to be 153 cm tall.

Combining the information available from crania and femora, the two burials can be sorted as follows. Burial 11 contained at least two individuals: 11A, of unknown sex, and 11B, possibly a female. If the two femora (F6 and F10) do not belong to 11B (It is certain they do not belong to 11A), then there are at least three individuals present. Burial 6 includes a child under age 11 (6C), and at least two adults, one male, and one female, as identified from femora. The large number of tibiae shown in the field notes of B-42 (most of them disintegrated in the field) lends support to the idea that the remaining two or three individuals belong to Burial 6.

No burial pit could be defined for the badly disturbed Burial 6. The burial included at least one extended individual (6A) and a bundle comprised of several individuals. B-6A was oriented with the head to the east-southeast. The only artifacts were a piece of shell and a bannerstone located about a foot to the south of skull 6A.

Burial 7 (July 1966; 5N/22E). Burial 7 was the easternmost burial in the cemetery. It was buried in an oval pit 5.2 ft. by 3.8 ft. and was oriented with the cranial end of the skeleton to the southeast. The legs and pelvis were articulated, but the right humerus was under the right tibia, the skull was between the knees (facing up with the crown towards the pelvis), the mandible was just to the left of the left femur, and most of the other bones were missing. Since both the skull and the femora were from a female, it was assumed that they belonged to the same individual. She was estimated to be about 32 years old. Her skull showed a slight amount of occipital flattening. The burial was fairly well-preserved and was undisturbed. The pit fill included burned bone, many sherds, and a broken deer effigy head from a pot.

Burials 8 and 9 (July 1966; 1S/32W). Although they were labeled separately in the field, B-8 and B-9 constituted a single, badly potted burial. Only two individuals were recognized in the field, but a total of at least four individuals can be accounted for from dental and cranial remains examined in the lab. Seven femur fragments representing six femora from three individuals belonged to two males and one female. Some bones were missing, particularly the fore-arms and the hands, but this can be attributed to the activities of the looters. B-8A was a 42-year-old adult of indeterminate sex who probably was buried in an extended position with his head to the east-southeast, facing up. Two deer ulna awls, a beaver tooth gouge, and three projectile points were placed next to the skull. Individual B was an adult aged about 30 years old, and C was a child about 6 years old. These two were identified in the lab. Burial 8D (formerly B-9) was a 40-year-old-male, and may have been part of a bundle with B and C. The pit fill included a few sherds.

Burial 10 (July or August 1966). The burial notes and map for B-10 have been lost for quite some time. Very few bone fragments from B-10 were found in the lab: two metatarsals, a metacarpal, a left clavicle piece, and part of a fibula. No more than one individual is represented by these fragments, and none of the bones used for figuring minimum counts for the cemetery were present.

Burial 11. See Burial 6.

Burial 12 (August 1966; 7S/23W). B-12 was badly disturbed and the bone was poorly preserved. It included two individuals who appeared to be extended with their heads pointed slightly south of east. Individual A was on the south or left side of B. Cranial fragments facing north were found for only one individual of indeterminate sex, probably 12A. Fragments of the pelvis of A were recovered, but could not be sexed. Both A and B were represented by legs; the legs of A crossed B's legs near the ankles. The legs of B were themselves crossed, right over left. Both individuals were determined to be female from the femoral circumference. Individual A was estimated to be 168 cm tall. A shallow bowl found about 2.5 ft. northeast of the skull of A may have been associated with the burial. The fill included some pot sherds, burned clay, and deer bone.

Burial 13 (August 1966; 7S/10E) (Pls. 2 and 3). An undisturbed multiple burial containing five individuals was found in the eastern part of the cemetery. Three of the burials were extended side-by-side with their heads pointed west. Individual A was the northernmost, B was central, and C was on the south side of the burial. A bundle containing two individuals lay atop the legs and pelvis of C. The bundle was arranged with the long bones in the middle and with the crania of D and E at the east and west ends. It is possible that the excavators may have confused some of the leg bones of C with those of D and E. All of the skulls faced south, except A, which faced north. The skull of C was undeformed (Pl. 7). Individuals A, B, and C were sexed by cranial morphology. A and B were also sexed by pelvic form. All three are females. D and E could not be sexed from the remains located in the lab, but the field notes listed one as male and one as female. Individual A was about 15 years old, B was about 46 years old, and C was 37 years old. Two male femora are attributed to C, but they probably belonged to D or E. They came from an adult about 166 cm tall. B was estimated to be 158 cm tall.

A surprising number of bones was missing from these skeletons considering that preservation was not so poor that large bones would disintegrate. No ribs were mapped for any of the burials, nor were any recognized in the lab. None of the extended individuals had a complete humerus or scapula. Only A had any vertebrae, and C lacked a pelvis. D and E were represented in the lab by a single pair of tibia shafts and distal humeri in addition to the misidentified femora attributed to C. The crania of D and E could not be located in the lab, although a box of cranial fragments incorrectly attributed to A but probably belonging to D or E was found. These fragments include teeth from an individual about 16 years old. They have been arbitrarily assigned to D, since no other remains of D or E can be sorted out to enable a positive identification.

A rattle was found at the left knee of A. A tool kit including two granite ground stone adzes, two deer ulna awls, and four utilized chert flakes was found at the feet of A and B. B also had a short-necked bottle to the left of her skull and a smaller long-necked bottle by her right shoulder. A projectile point was located roughly a foot west of her skull. Individual 13C had a small effigy bowl (without the head) to the right of her skull and a bear claw and some shell near her right arm.

Burial 14 (August 1966). The only bone recovered from B-14 was a smashed child's cranium without teeth. It was accompanied by a short-necked bottle resting above a small flaring rim bowl. The provenience of this burial is unknown.

Burial 15 (August 1966; 21N/23W) (Pl. 4). A 41-year-old female was buried with a dog on the north side of the cemetery. Her sex was determined from pelvic and cranial morphology. She was oriented with her head pointing to the east-southeast, facing right. Her right leg was extended, and her left leg was flexed, with the heel drawn up to the right knee. The right hand was at her chin, while the elbow was at her side. The left arm was flexed underneath the dog. The dog was flexed and lying on its left side, except for the skull, which lay on its right side. The burial was discovered by a pothunter who lost some of the bones in his excavation. The woman's vertebrae were completely disintegrated, but the cranial fragments and the femora were in fairly good condition. Her skull was undeformed. She was estimated to have been 163 cm tall. No artifacts were found with the burial by the pothunters or the archaeologists.

Burial 16 (August 1966; 12N/21W). Burial 16 was a poorly preserved, undisturbed bundle burial containing two individuals found south of Burial 15. The burial pit could not be defined, but the bundle was aligned on an east-west axis with a skull at either end. The burial map shows two dentitions, but only one set of teeth was found in the lab. These belonged to a 26-year-old male with an undeformed skull who will be called Individual A. A few of the long bones survived to reach the lab. Among them was the shaft of a woman's right femur. This femur, F-1, is presumed to belong to 16B. No artifacts were found with the burial.

Burial 17. See Burial 38.

Burial 18 (August 1966; 11S/28W) (Pl. 5). Burial 18 was a badly disturbed multiple burial. The excavators identified a minimum of three individuals; two represented by overlapped, extended legs, and one represented by a bundle of long bones and a cranium. The heads of the extended individuals would have pointed east. Individual A was on the south and had the left leg of B between her legs. The bundle was on the north side of the burial near the right knee of B. A total of four females was identified in the lab from femora and tibiae. Cranial fragments included the skull and mandible of Individual C and another unidentified mandible. C was about 57 years old, while the other mandible (probably from D) was from a 25-year-old. B-18A was about 151 cm tall. A number of osteophytic vertebrae were recovered from the bundle.

Burial 19 (August 1966; 2S/13E). An extended burial, Individual B, with a skull, Individual A, by the left arm was found on the eastern edge of the cemetery. Individual B was an adult female oriented with her head to the east and facing left. Her cranium could not be found in the lab; her sex was determined from her femoral circumference. Individual A was a 9.5-year-old with the crown of the head pointed west, facing up. Preservation was poor, although the burial was undisturbed. A shallow bowl was found just inches east of the adult's head. There was a perforated-based, long-necked bottle at the side of the burial.

Burial 20 (July 1968; 9N/47W). A single extended individual was the westernmost burial in the cemetery. The burial pit was an oval 7.4 ft. by 2.9 ft. and shared an east-southeast orientation with the skeleton. B-20 was determined to be a male from cranial form. He was about 44 years old and was about 173 cm tall. His skull showed a heavy degree of intentional occipital flattening. According to the field notes, a flint flake was found lodged in the left ribs. The excavator thought it may have been an arrow point, and that it represented an injury inflicted upon B-20. The burial had been probed by pothunters, but was otherwise undisturbed and in good condition. The pit fill included charred corn, sherds and deer bone.

Burial 21 (August 1972; 12S/2W). Burial 21 contained two extended individuals with their heads to the east. Preservation was very poor, and two historical disturbances aggravated the situation. The burial was potted on the north side, probably in 1966. Then, after the burial was exposed, but before the bones had been removed, several youths rode mini-bikes over the bones. Considering this, it is amazing that anything can be learned from B-21. The pit was about 8.4 ft. long and 4.5 ft. wide and was oriented east-west. Individual A, an adult male, was represented by fragments from the head to the pelvis. To the left of A was B, an adult female represented by a few vertebrae and some pelvic and leg fragments. Burial 21A was sexed by cranial and pelvic form; 21B was sexed by femoral circumference. The cranium of A was undeformed. The fill in the burial pit included debris from the village.

Burial 22 (August 1972; 34S/33W). The southernmost burial of the cemetery was a poorly preserved, undisturbed, bundle burial containing three persons. Individual A was a 42-year-old male with a heavily flattened occiput. The post-cranial bones in the burial are most likely his. A stature of about 172 cm is calculated from his femora. B is an adult of indeterminate sex represented only by cranial fragments. C is a child of about five years represented by some cranial bone and teeth. The burial pit could not be defined. No artifacts were found in association with the burial, but village debris was included in the fill.

Burial 23 (August 1972; 32S/32W). A single, complete, extended skeleton in fair condition was recovered adjacent to B-22. The pit of B-23 was 7.4 ft. by 2.0 ft. and was oriented on a west-northwest by east-southeast axis. The burial was determined to be male from examination of the pelvis. He was 25 years old and about 170 cm tall. He was oriented with his head to the east-southeast, facing up. The cranium showed an intermediate degree of occipital deformation. No artifacts were recovered, but a possible pothole was discerned at the right elbow. Village debris was found in the fill.

Burial 24 (August 1972; 28S/30W). North of B-23 was a burial pit 9 ft. by 3.6 ft. which was believed to contain the remains of three individuals. B-24A was extended with its shattered cranium to the east-southeast. The skull of B was at his left shoulder, and the bundle containing C was to the right of his legs. The skull of A was evidently damaged by pothunters. The excavators did not properly separate the bones, so that B-24A as uncovered in the lab had two right temporals. Further work showed that teeth and mandible fragments had been confused between A and B, and that Individual C was really two people. With the aid of the burial map, the confusion has been reduced, but not ended completely. Although it is possible to identify four distinct frontals, they can not be definitely associated with their temporals or their post-cranial skeletons. B was represented only by cranial fragments and can not be sexed, but was about thirty-one-years old. B-24A was an old male, but could not be aged because too few molars were available. Individiduals C and D were aged 36 and 39 respectively. Both were sexed female from their femoral circumferences. The post-cranial skeletons of Individuals C and D were not completely represented, but historic disturbance might be responsible for this, since it is hard to believe that even the most inept field archaeologist could mix the remains as thoroughly as they were. B-24A was about 166 cm tall, and either C or D was 164 cm tall. No artifacts were reported with the burial, although occupational debris was incorporated in the pit fill.

Burial 25 (August 25S/29W). Two individuals were extended in an 8.0 ft. by 2.8 ft. pit to the north of B-24. Individual A was six years old, and Individual B was estimated to be 43 years old. The adult was determined to be a female from pelvic and cranial form. Both skeletons were extended with their heads to the east-southeast. The female was to the left of the child and faced left. The burial was undisturbed and preservation was fair, so a number of the post-cranial bones of the child were recovered. B-25A was estimated to be 151 cm tall. Her skull was undeformed. No artifacts were associated with the burials.

Burial 26 (August 1972; 21S/28W). A single extended adult male was buried north of B-25. Sex was determined from femoral circumference. He was oriented with his fragmentary cranium to the east-southeast. Although preservation was only fair, and the burial had been potted, it was apparent that the burial had been completely articulated. B-26 was an individual about 164 cm tall. No artifacts were found with the burial, but the shaft of the right femur of another adult male was found above the right shoulder. The femur was probably introduced through the pothole that smashed the skull. A few of the thoracic vertebrae of B-26 were compressed and showed osteophytic lipping.

Burial 27 (August 1972; 16S/27W). Burial 27 was a poorly preserved single interment extended with its head to the east-southeast. The legs were crossed at the ankles, left over right. Examination of the sciatic notch showed this to be a female. She was about 54 years old. From the burial map, it appears that the skull lay on its left side. The mandible was by the left shoulder, but the rest of the skeleton was articulated. The mandible fragment could have been removed by a rodent or a pothunter. The cranium showed an intermediate amount of occipital flattening. No artifacts were associated with the burial.

Burial 28 (August 1972; 2S/24W). Three individuals were buried in a pit 5.4 ft. by 2.9 ft. to the east of B-8. B-28A was extended with its head to the east-southeast, and B and C may have been another example of a bundle with the skulls at either end and long bones in the middle. A laboratory worker mistakenly mixed the bones of the three skeletons together. This accident made it impossible to identify the bones belonging to any particular individual. Only one mandible could be partially reconstructed, so this was arbitrarily called "A" for the purposes of this report. Individual A was about 15.5 years old. All three individuals were identified as females from their femoral circumferences. An extra right femur fragment from a male was also found in the burial. It is the only evidence of a fourth person, and may represent extraneous bone accidently introduced. The bones were in a terrible state of preservation, but were probably undisturbed. A bone needle was found mixed in with some ribs in the lab. No artifacts were mentioned in the field notes.

Burial 29 (August 1972; 2N/21W). Burial 29 was a 5-year-old child buried in a pit 5.3 ft. by 2.0 ft. The cranium was at the southeast end of the pit, lying on its left side. Preservation was fair and much of the vertebral column was recovered. No long bones were found, but a few ribs remained under the mandible. The south side of this burial pit overlaps the pit of B-37. A celt was found with the child.

Burial 30 (August 1972; 7N/15W). The poorly preserved, undisturbed, extented skeleton of an adult was oriented with the head west in a pit 5.5 ft. by 2.5 ft. It was determined to be a female from femoral circumference. She was 50 years old. No artifacts were associated with her.

Burials 31 and 50 (August 1972 and June 1973; 2S/13W). A poorly preserved multiple burial located at the center of the cemetery was excavated during two field seasons. It was not realized until the final cemetery map was made that Burials 31 and 50 were part of the same burial. This discovery resolved a few problems, since B-50, an adult skeleton with a child's cranium was difficult to explain. The child's skull belonged to the skeleton 31B. The adult skeleton from B-50 has been renamed 31C. The three skeletons were extended with their heads to the east-southeast. Individual A was on the south, B was in the middle, and C was on the north. B-31A was a headless adult female who was sexed by femoral circumference. B was a fairly complete 6-year-old. C was an adult male, missing from the waist up, who was sexed by pelvic form. The missing crania may be the result of the depredations of the pothunters. In addition to some unburned clay found in the pit, a granite adze was found to the right of C.

A Scallorn point (cf. Bell 1960:84) was found imbedded in the left innominate of C. The point was in the ischium just below the junction with the ilium. Dr. Louise Robbins (personal communication: October 30, 1973) of North Carolina State University examined the innominate and expressed the opinion that the point became imbedded after the death of C. Her opinion was based primarily on the fact that the bone appeared to have been disturbed post-mortem, so that there was no way to be certain the point was not introduced during that disturbance. She did note that the central foveal area of the acetabulum showed pathological symptoms possibly relating to the injury or destruction of the femoral ligament. Unknown to her, it was possible to date definitely at least one post-mortem disturbance of the innominate. When it was removed from the ground, it broke open, revealing the projectile point. Clumsy attempts at repair may well be responsible for the disturbances to the bone which caused her to be restrained in her evaluation of the innominate. It is assumed here that the point was introduced into the pelvis through the agency of an arrow shot from a bow. This type of injury was not unique to B-31C in the Powers phase. B-1 from Powers Fort sustained a similar injury, and B-20 from Turner may also have been wounded.

Burial 32 (August 1972; 13S/17W). A poorly preserved adult female was buried in a 6.0 ft. by 2.5 ft. pit to the south of B-31. The legs were loosely flexed with the knees to the right. The burial map gives the impression that the trunk was in the usual supine position with the head to the east-southeast. Unfortunately, the cranium had been removed by looters. Sex was determined from femoral circumference. The pit was 6.0 ft. by 2.5 ft. No artifacts were recovered by the archaeologists.

Burial 33 (August 1972; 30S/44W). Three individuals were buried in a pit 8.5 ft. by 4.8 ft. in the southwest corner of the cemetery. The bones were in a fair state of preservation and were undisturbed. Individuals A and B were determined to be males from pelvic and cranial morphology. They were extended with their heads to the east-southeast, and with B to the left of A. On the map, the skull of A appears to overlap that of B. The cranium of B-33C, a child about six years old, lay on its left side facing east-southeast well above the left femur of B. This skull may have been added to the burial after the initial interment. B-33A was about 23 years old and stood 174 cm tall. B was considerably older, but lacked sufficient teeth to be aged. He was about 169 cm tall. B-33C had an extremely flattened occiput, while A showed this trait to a lesser degree, and B was undeformed. No grave goods were found with the burials, although some sherds and deer bones were found in the pit fill.

Burial 34 (August 1972; 22S/41W). The single burial of a 27-year-old female was found just north of B-33. She was extended with her head northwest in a pit 6.6 ft. by 3.6 ft. Her sex was determined from pelvic and cranial form. The burial was probably disturbed, since part of the dentition was missing and part was found above skull. The rest of the skeleton appears to have been completely articulated, although poor preservation causes a degree of uncertainty. A tool kit consisting of three shells, three hammerstones, one celt, and the broken sherds of a small jar was found about six inches to the north of her left shoulder.

Burial 35 (August 1972; 19S/32W). An undisturbed multiple burial was excavated from a 6.0 ft. by 2.8 ft. pit to the north of B-34. The remains included three fairly preserved adult females who were extended with their heads to the east-southeast. A few fragments of a child's cranium were found with the pelvis of 35B. Individual A was on the north side of the burial, with B slightly overlapping her. C was to the left of B. Individuals A and B were sexed on the basis of cranial and pelvic form, but C could be sexed only by femoral circumference. B-35A, B, and C are estimated to be aged 20, 38, and 33 years, respectively. The child was probably under age two, judging from the thickness of the cranial vault. The only pathology observed was the osteophytic lipping of some of the thoracic vertebrae of B. B was estimated to be 153 cm tall, while A was 155 cm. A knife was found at the right shoulder of A, a point base at the knees of B, and a shallow bowl over B's mandible. The usual village debris was incorporated in the fill.

Burial 36 (August 1972; 4N/12W). Burial 36 was a disturbed double burial in a pit about 6 ft. by 4 ft. located next to B-30. Both individuals were aligned with their heads to the east-southeast. Individual B, on the right, was a 21-year-old female about 152 cm tall with an undeformed skull. Her age is based not only on tooth wear, but also on the fact that the iliac crest was unfused near the sacral articulation. This corresponds to Stage 2 of union (McKern and Stewart 1957) and represents an age of 17 to 22 or younger. Individual A was a 28-year-old male about 172 cm tall. Both individuals were sexed by pelvic and cranial morphology. A third individual was represented by right femur and tibia fragments found in the lab in a bag labeled 36C. These fragments were never seen or identified with the burial in the field. Perhaps a bag of bones from another burial was mislabeled. Only scattered sherds and animal bone fragments were found with the burial, although Dale Turner, who farms the land, claimed that 11 pots were removed here by thieves. Since pothunters seldom completely expose a burial, his attribution of the pots to this particular burial may be in error.

Burial 37 (August 1972; 1S/21W). Two poorly preserved individuals were recovered from a pit 6.2 ft. by 2.0 ft. south of B-29. Individual B was an extended adult female oriented with her head to the east-southeast. B-37A was the skull of a 2-year-old placed at the right elbow of B. B was sexed by her femoral circumference. Pothunters smashed the skull of B in their search for artifacts. No artifacts were found with the burials.

Burials 38 and 17 (August 1972 and August 1966; 12S/37W). A disturbed burial was recovered from the west side of the cemetery. Burial 17 was probably extended with the head to the east-southeast, but it is difficult to be certain since the only long bones clearly illustrated on the burial map were those of one arm. If the arm was aligned with the trunk, then the skull was oriented with the crown towards the trunk (west-northwest) and facing south. A thin streak of charcoal passed under the skull. Beneath the maxilla was the right temporal of another individual. The mandible was disarticulated and located about 6 in. east of the skull. A decorated jar was located a half foot south of the skull, and a projectile point was about 3 in. to the north of the skull. A creek rock was found another 6 in. east of the mandible. The undeformed cranium is feminine in form.

When B-17 was plotted on the cemetery map, it appeared that it may have been part of B-38. The two burials do not line up perfectly, but this may be explained by the fact that they were mapped on separate alidade maps six years apart. B-17 lacked legs, while B-38 had a paucity of skeletal material from above the waist. The feet of B-38 pointed to the west-northwest. Five pairs of legs were identified in the field for B-38. They were lying side-by-side with some overlap and were labeled A, B, C, D, and E from the north to the south. The right leg of E lay under the left leg of C. The left leg of D was between the legs of E, and the right leg was between C's legs. From the field map, it is unclear whether D was above or beneath C and E. If B-17 belonged to one of these sets of legs, it was probably B-38E. The femur of E was that of a female, perhaps not fully grown. B-17 was a female about 16 years old. A pothole was mapped to the north of B-17, right where two potholes were located in B-38. It will be assumed that B-17 was the same individual as B-38E, and the B-17 designation will be abandoned. The extra temporal fragment from B-17 will be called B-38 CF-2. The adult cranial fragments and teeth already identified for B-38 must have belonged to either B or C, since A and D were juveniles. The child's teeth from the burial belonged to A or D. In sum, the five individuals of B-38 were: A and D, children, one of whom is 5.5 years old; B, an adult female; C, an adult; and E, a young female. A segment of a man's left femur was found in a loose bone bag in the lab. This may represent a sixth person or it may have belonged to C. It will be assumed that it belonged to C. Burial 38 is in terrible condition. The excavators thought that two individuals were present in a bundle with the five extended individuals, but it is more likely that this is the disturbed portion of the burial. The fill included a few sherds, a cone fragment (Price 1973:46), and some sandstone.

Burial 39 (August 1972; 8S/16W). The poorly preserved cranium of a child was found north of B-32. No artifacts were found in association. Since the cranium was never located in the lab in Ann Arbor, it was not included in the minimum parts inventory in Appendix C.

Burial 40 (June 1973; 4N/20W). A badly disturbed, extended burial was excavated just north of B-29. Femoral circumference indicated that this was a female. She was extended with her head to the east-southeast. Her skull showed a slight amount of occipital flattening. The burial pit was poorly defined, but was approximately 6.6 ft. by 3.5 ft. Jar sherds were found in the fill.

Burial 41 (June 1973; 13S/25W). Burial 41 was described in the field notes as a single extended burial, located west of B-40. The burial pit was listed on the field notes as 3.4 ft. by 2.0 ft. Unless the disturbance of the burial was more severe than usually was the case, it is more likely that this was a bundle burial. Furthermore, the remains of two individuals were present. B-41A was a child represented by cranial fragments. The development of the occipital suggests an age of about eight to 12 years. B-41B was an adult female represented by a few well worn maxillary teeth and some long bones. She lacked sufficient teeth to be aged by dental wear. Her sex was determined from her femoral circumference. These femora show evidence of an old trauma according to Dr. Andrew Poznanski of the Mott Children's Hospital of the University of Michigan. No artifacts were recovered.

Burial 42. See Burial 6.

Burial 43 (June 1973; 8N/32W). Fragments of the poorly preserved right femur and innominate of an adult were found north of B-6. If this represented an extended burial, the skull would have been to the east. It is likely that most of the burial had been plowed or potted out. The bone was in such poor condition that it could not be removed from the ground and taken to the lab. It does not appear on the laboratory inventory sheet in Appendix C for this reason.

Burial 44 (June 1973; 10N/29W). Another poorly preserved individual was recovered from a disturbed burial north of B-43. The remains consisted of a few cranial fragments, parts of the left femur and innominate, a piece of the right humerus, and a tibia fragment. The remains appeared to have been oriented with the head west-northwest. This was an adult of indeterminate sex. The base of a very poor quality bowl was found near the cranial fragments.

Burial 45 (June 1973; 14N/8W). An extended adult female was excavated south of B-3. Her sex was determined from her femoral circumference. The fragments of her disturbed cranium were oriented to the east-southeast.

Preservation was poor, but the situation was aggravated by prolonged exposure of the burial before the bone was removed. The dirt around the burial became so hard that a dental pick was broken in the attempt to dislodge some of the bone. Although both legs, the trunk, the arms, and cranial fragments were identified in the field, few of these survived to be returned to the lab. The only cranial fragment that was recovered was the right gonial angle of the mandible. The pit fill included a few sherds and a raccoon maxilla which had heavily worn M^2 and M^3.

Burial 46 (June 1973; 2N/3W). The badly disturbed burial of an adult male was uncovered east of B-36. Part of the disturbance may have been related to excavations in search of the permanent site datum at the beginning of several field seasons. B-46 was extended with his shoulders to the west-northwest. His head was missing, so he had to be sexed by femoral circumference. A possible tool kit of an arrowshaft abrader and several pieces of worked chert were located in the vicinity of the pelvis. A few sherds and pieces of deer bone were included in the fill.

Burial 47 (June 1973; 1S/7W). South of B-46 was an adult female extended with her head west. Her legs were crossed, left over right, in a fashion reminiscent of the "modest lady" of Funkhouser and Webb (1931: Fig. 14). Her sex was determined from her femoral circumference. The burial pit was about 5.9 ft. by 2.4 ft. Her bones were all present, except for the smaller ones which had disintegrated. She was 34 years old and about 162 cm tall. Her skull showed an intermediate degree of occipital flattening. Dr. William Martel of the University of Michigan Hospitals examined the femora and said they may show evidence of an old trauma. The pit fill contained the usual village debris—shell, bone, sherds, and chert flakes. There may have been other artifacts located at her feet where there were potholes.

Burial 48 (June 1973; 6S/5W). A badly disturbed but fairly preserved adult female was buried south of B-47. She was extended with her few remaining cranial fragments to the east-southeast in a pit 6.0 ft. by 2.2 ft. The pit dimensions may have been altered by the excavations of vandals. Sex was determined from her pelvic morphology. Her stature was approximately 152 cm. The pit fill included deer bone, chert flakes, and a few fragments from a ceramic cone object.

Burial 49 (June 1973; 8S/6W). Another badly disturbed burial in fair to poor condition was uncovered south of B-48. An old female was extended with her head west-northwest in a pit 6.0 ft. by 2.9 ft. Her skull was difficult to assign to either sex because she had fairly heavy supraorbital ridges and a thick vault, but small mastoid and zygomatic processes. The sciatic notch was very wide, however, and provided the "swing vote" in the determination of the sex. The woman stood about 155 cm tall. Another individual of indeterminate sex was represented by a distal fragment of the left femur. This piece of bone (F-2) was probably introduced through a pothole. No artifacts were recovered.

Burial 50. See Burial 31.

Burial 51 (June 1973). An extended male in fair condition was found with his head to the east-southeast on the west side of the cemetery. Sex was determined from cranial form. Since his legs were missing, the measured length of 5.0 ft. for the pit was probably incorrect. It was 2.2 ft. wide. B-51 was about 38 years old and had an undeformed skull. His legs had probably been plowed out of the burial. No artifacts were found.

Burial 52 (June 1973; 5S/34W). Burial 52 was poorly preserved and badly disturbed, particularly at its eastern end. Although the pit could not be defined, the bone scatter was about 6.8 ft. by 2.0 ft. It contained a minimum of five individuals. Three adults and one child were represented by cranial fragments, and a fourth adult was represented by long bones. One individual, a female, was represented by articulated legs (F-2 and F-7) and would have had her head to the east-southeast. She was probably complete and extended before the burial was ripped up by looters. Other bones were found to be partly articulated, but there were never enough to allow burial position to be determined. Furthermore, they could not be assigned to particular individuals. Cranial fragments were found at both ends and at the middle of the burial. A calotte (CF-1), punctured by eight probe holes, appears to have come from a male. It was found in the vicinity of the pelvis of the extended female. No pelvic fragments could be sexed, but femora could be paired and then sexed. A second female was represented by a lone left femur (F-3), and two males were identified from femur pairs F-1 and F-6, F-4 and F-5. The child, 52A, was estimated to be about 11 years old from the calcification of several loose mandibular and maxillary teeth. Three adults of indeterminate sex were aged by dental attrition. B-52B was 22, D was 35, and C was 55. From the way the bones were piled around the east end of the burial, it seems likely that at least two, and perhaps three, of the individuals were in a bundle on the chest of the extended female. One individual in the bundle must be male, but the sex of the other is uncertain. An articulated left tibia and fibula pair to the right of the legs of the extended female and properly aligned and separated from a left humerus may represent another extended adult, but there is no way to be sure. Stature could be determined for all the adults except the extended female. The males were

164 cm and 174 cm tall, and the other female was 153 cm tall. A Scallorn point was found under the distal end of Femur 5 (the short male). The only other artifacts recovered were sherds and chert flakes.

Burial 53 (June 1973; ON/7E). Two poorly preserved females were placed in a double bundle burial in the eastern part of the cemetery. It is difficult to tell whether the burial was disturbed. The pit was 4.2 ft. long and 2.3 ft. wide, with the long axis oriented east-southeast by west-northwest. The crania were placed at the ends of the bundle with two pairs of crossed long bones between them. The eastern pair of crossbones was composed of right and left femora. The western pair was composed of a right tibia and a right femur. The other left femur was located in the main mass of bones underneath the crossed pairs. Also in the mass of bones were a few small cranial fragments and two teeth from A. Neither mandible was present. Both individuals were sexed by their cranial form. In addition, a female pelvis was recognized. The eastern female, Individual A, was about 29 years old, while B was 52 years old. A small hollow pocket was visible in the broken frontal of B. Dr. Andrew Poznanski of the Mott Children's Hospital at the University of Michigan examined this specimen and its X-ray. He believes that the pocket was a small epidermoid cyst. Two chert flakes and a bone needle were included in the bundle.

Burial 54 (June 1973; 16N/26W). Burial 54 was composed of two small clusters of bone located south of B-15. Although it was in line with a row of burials, it is not clear whether this burial was more representative of the work of pothunters or of the Powers phase people. Except for a distal fragment of a left femur, only cranial bone is present. Other than a section of occipital and adjacent left and right temporals (CF-1), the bone was in poor condition. There certainly is not enough bone to put together one complete skull, let alone the three which were represented. The restored occipital (CF-1) was probably from a male. Among the teeth in B-54 were two left maxillary fourth premolars, so at least two individuals were represented by teeth. Only one of them, B-54A, a 22-year-old of unknown sex, could be aged. One flake, a nut shell, and a cluster of sherds were found in the area. B-54 will be omitted from the counts of individuals done on a burial-by-burial basis in Appendix B, since these individuals may be represented elsewhere.

Burial 55 (July 1973; 23N/22W). A badly disturbed scatter of bones occupying an area 7.8 ft. long by 3.7 ft. wide was found north of B-15. At least five individuals, including two juveniles, were present in the burial. A child's skull in very poor condition was recovered from the west end of the burial, just to the west of a set of deer antlers. This child, B-55A lacked any teeth and so could not be aged, except very roughly by the development of the petrous part of the temporal. An age under eight years seems reasonable. Another child's skull, B-55B, was found near the west end of the burial. It was lying on its right side, facing north. B-55B was about 5.5 years old when he died. Two adult males, C and D were identified and aged from mandibles. C was 32, D was 34. One of them was also represented by his femora and by pelvic fragments (P-1). A female was identified from pelvic fragments (P-2) and from femora, but no teeth or cranial fragments could be definitely attributed to her. Several sets of articulated bones could have come from extended burials. A left arm was articulated and appeared on the burial map just to the south of the child's skull B. Also appearing on the map, just east of the deer antlers, was an articulated lower leg. To the right of this leg were articulated left and right feet. These probably represent two individuals. If so, one was certainly male, while the other could have been either sex. No other articulated bones were recovered. The skull of B was probably laid on the chest of the individual represented by the articulated arm. The adult cranial bones and teeth were scattered widely in the potted areas of the burial. The pathological material from the burial included one compressed, osteophytic vertebra and a tibia with an unusually rectangular cross-section. Other than the antlers, the recovered artifacts included a small hammerstone, a Scallorn point, some ochre, and the usual village debris.

Burial 56 (July 1973; 27N/18W). A poorly preserved child's cranium was found north of B-55. It was lying on its left side facing northwest, at the southeast end of a pit 3.4 ft. wide and 5.0 ft. long. The pit was oriented on a southeast-northwest axis. A few fragments of bone which may have been part of the post-cranial skeleton disintegrated as they were excavated. The child was about 2.5 years old. The right half of the skull was missing and may have been disked away. To the east of the head, in a rodent burrow, were an Archaic point, a few sherds, and a rock. Several sherds, some charcoal flecks, a chunk of quartzite, and a piece of deer bone were found in the pit fill.

Burial 57 (July 1973; 7N/30W). A child's very poorly preserved mandible was found along with a few crumbling teeth and a cranial fragment to the east of B-43. B-57 was aged slightly less than two years at death. No other traces of this burial were found, and it is unclear whether this represented a primary or a secondary interment. Several chert flakes were scattered in the vicinity.

Burial 58 (July 1973; 25N/10W). A pile of fairly well preserved bone was dumped into a pothole north of B-1. Although assigned a burial number for convenience of reference, this was not a burial created by the Turner inhabitants. A chunk of attached occipital and parietal were probably from a male. Also found were a left mandible fragment with heavily worn canine and third premolar (the posterior teeth were lost antemortem), a right femur shaft from a female, a tibia fragment, and a fragment of a right humerus. This could have been more of the potted burial, B-2, but because that burial was never mapped, there is no way to know, and B-58 must be considered separately. When minimum individuals are counted on a burial-by-burial basis in Appendix B, B-58 will be ignored since it may include individuals represented elsewhere.

Burial 59 (July 1973; 34N/3W). The northernmost burial of the cemetery was a 7.5-year-old child who was extended with his head to the east. The burial pit was 4.5 ft. by 3.1 ft. and showed the same orientation. Fragments of his femora, tibiae, humeri, and ribs were recognized in the field, but few survived to reach the lab. Sherds, flakes, seed hulls, charcoal, and deer bone were found in the fill.

Burial 60 (August 1973; 12N/1W). An old male was extended with his head west-northwest to the east of B-45. He was facing up with both forearms pronated and his left leg crossed over the right at mid-tibia. His undeformed skull was in fair condition, except for having been perforated by a dozen probe holes. The rest of the burial was badly deteriorated. No maxillary teeth were found, but the anterior part of the maxilla had been eroded. The following teeth were definitely lost antemortem, as evidenced by the resorption of the alveolar bone: $RM^3M^2M^1$, $LM^3M^2M^1$, $RM_3M_2M_1P_4P_3$, $LM_3M_2M_1$. He stood about 168 cm tall. His atlas showed osteophytic lipping around the facet for the odontoid process. An inferior quality bowl was found to the west of his right shoulder, and a few sherds and a flake were in the fill.

Burial 61. As explained in Chapter One, there was no Burial 61. Instead, this designation pertains to a collection of human bones stored in plaster casts in the basement of the Powers Phase Project headquarters in Naylor, Missouri. Moisture destroyed the casts and their labels, and no one could recall anything of their contents, except that they had been excavated at Turner in 1966. They can no longer be attributed to any particular burial, since the remains from several casts were commingled when the casts fell apart. Surprisingly, the bone was fairly well preserved.

Seven adults were identified on the basis of five femur pairs and two right femora. Five of these were females, and two were males. Of the five left and three right innominate fragments, three (two left, one right) could be sexed. Those three were female and came from only two individuals (P-1 and P-2). Five individuals were identified from cranial fragments, and five were identified from mandibles. Only B-61A, a 20-year-old female, was represented by both the skull and dentition. The cranial fragments CF-2 and CF-3 were sufficiently complete to be sexed as female (CF-3 is shown in Pl. 6). The skull CF-2 was undeformed. The fragments CF-1 and CF-4 were too small to sex. The four remaining mandibles were from individuals aged about 32 (B), 20 (C), 48 (D), and 65 (E). Burial 61E is the oldest individual with an assigned age from Turner. Several loose maxillary teeth came from at least two individuals other than A, but could not be definitely paired with any mandible. Stature could be estimated for four individuals. The three females represented by the femur pairs F-1 and F-10, F-5 and F-8, and F-6 and F-9 were 158 cm, 153 cm, and 156 cm tall, respectively. The male represented by F-2 and F-11 was 160 cm tall. Two unusual tibiae from B-61 probably show the results of an old trauma, according to Dr. Andrew Poznanski of the Mott Children's Hospital of the University of Michigan. Burial 61 will be included in the tabulation of minimum individuals on a burial-by-burial basis in Appendix B, since it is comprised of several fairly complete burials.

STRAY FRAGMENTS

Numerous loose bone fragments were found in the lab in Ann Arbor at the bottom of a box containing casts from these burials: B-3, B-8, B-13A, B-13C, B-19, and perhaps others. Although many fragments could be correctly attributed, there were some leftovers. The largest was a male calotte thought to be from B-19 before it was realized that B-19 contained only a female and a child. This cranium showed an intermediate degree of occipital flattening. Among the other fragments were a frontal with small fragments of the parietals, an occipital with parietal fragments, and a large left parietal fragment. There were also several mandible fragments, including one with tooth roots, and a maxilla fragment which retained RM^1. Some loose teeth were also found in the box. The post-cranial remains included most of a left foot.

TURNER SURFACE COLLECTION

None of the fragments of the human bone recovered from the surface of the site could be assigned to any particular burial, even in a few cases where approximate provenience was recorded. The loose teeth included 21 maxillary and 16 mandibular teeth from individuals ranging in age from childhood to middle-aged adulthood. The other cranial and post-cranial materials appear in the inventory in Appendix C but are not included in the burial-by-burial minimum individuals count of Appendix B. Teeth are not included in the inventory in Appendix C, since no complete or partially complete dentitions are included, just loose teeth which almost certainly came from burials already included in the minimum mandible and maxilla counts.

The Snodgrass Site Human Remains

The excavation grid at Snodgrass was laid out from the Turner datum. No formal cemetery was found at Snodgrass.

Burial 1 (June 1968; 180S/950E). This was not so much a burial as it was a bone scatter left by pothunters. It was located south of Structure 88. Two individuals can be identified from the cranial fragments. However, neither can be reconstructed sufficiently to be aged or sexed. The occipital of CF-1 was complete enough to tell that it was slightly flattened. The post-cranial remains were also from a minimum of two individuals. At least one of these was a female, judging from the circumference of the left femur. No artifacts could be definitely associated with the bone scatter.

Burial 2 (July 1969; 146S/827E). The burial notes describe this as a young adult female. Since her remains could not be located in the lab, this could not be confirmed. The burial pit was near Structure 23 and the "white wall," a structure which surrounded 38 of the largest buildings on the Snodgrass site (Price 1973). She was extended with her head to the west-northwest. The head appears to be fragmentary in the illustration accompanying the burial notes, and her left tibia has been moved out of place. No remarks were made on the burial forms that would have indicated whether this was the result of prehistoric or modern activities on the site. The only artifacts were sherds from the pit fill.

Burial 3 (July 1970; 323S/927E). A 20-year-old female was extended in a 6.2 ft. by 2.0 ft. pit with her head to the north-northeast. The burial was located near the white wall and east of Structures 42 and 43. Its sex was determined from pelvic and cranial form. She stood about 166 cm tall and had an undeformed skull. The bone was in fairly good condition, and the burial was undisturbed. The associated artifacts included a small-mouthed jar and may have included a deer mandible and maxilla found nearby. An extra right patella was found in the lab in a bag which was labeled "vertebrae and sacrum," but which actually contained only the patella and a few nondescript fragments. The patella probably belongs to B-4A which was first exposed in 1970 on the last day of the field season. Only parts of B-4A were removed before the 1971 excavations. No right patella was found in the inventory of fragments identified as belonging to 4A, so this one is reassigned accordingly.

Burial 4 (August 1970 and July 1971; 179S/803E). The remains of an adult and a child were found under Structure 25. When the site burned, a section of the white wall collapsed into this house and covered B-4. The adult skeleton (A) was supine with the legs slightly flexed to the left and with the head oriented to the east-southeast and facing up. The left leg was missing. This was a 43-year-old male suffering from severe periodontal disease. His sex was determined from his cranial form. His skull showed an intermediate degree of occipital flattening. At his right hip was the tightly flexed skeleton of B, a 2-year-old child. The artifacts included a large rim sherd from a wide-mouthed jar which was near the child's skull, and a piece of gypsum found near the lumbar vertebrae of A.

Burial 5 (August 1970; 185S/839E). This burial should have been designated STR 19 B-1, since it was the burial of an infant beneath the floor of a house, Structure 19. No bone from a burial at this location has been found in the lab.

Burial 6 (August 1970; 162S/840E). This should have been designated STR 20 B-1. It was an infant burial. No field notes were taken other than the provenience. No remains were found in the lab.

Burial 7 (August 1971; 106S/890E). A 22-year-old female was extended with her head to the east-southeast and facing north between Structures 63, 64, and 89. Her sex was determined from her pelvic and cranial form. She was about 160 cm tall. The burial had been disturbed by modern agricultural practices and by rodents, but the bone was in fair to good condition. A scalloped-rim bowl was found just south of her undeformed cranium, and a small-mouthed jar rested on her chest beneath her mandible. The burial pit was 6.6 ft. by 2.2 ft. and was oriented along the same axis as the burial.

Burial 8 (August and September 1973; 283S/947E). Fragments of an adult skeleton were found near the white wall at the bottom of Extra-edificial Pit 92. The remains were found in three clusters: the left ulna, radius, and humerus and a few loose teeth; the right metatarsals and phalanges; and a scapula and clavicle. Because the bones within each cluster were articulated when they were found, there is the possibility that this represents a fully articulated burial which was disturbed either accidentally or intentionally during the aboriginal occupation of the site. However, the bones of the pectoral girdle were found 4 ft. from the humerus cluster and just 3 ft. from the metatarsal cluster, which is 5 ft. from the arm cluster. This raises the possibility that the body was partially disarticulated before burial. Unfortunately, the poorly preserved bones from this burial remain in Missouri. Associated artifacts included a short-necked water bottle about 3.5 ft. south of the arm; a deer skull, some galena, and some hematite near the shoulder bones; a piece of galena, a quartz crystal, and an ear plug with the arm bones.

Structure 19 Burned (August 1970; 185S/830E). The burned, fragmentary remains of an adult were found in Structure 19 in a scatter 10 ft. by 6 ft. Two pieces of frontal that fit together were found 4 ft. apart. The cranial fragments were burned to a metallic hardness. They are white to blue-white in color along recent break lines. Most are cracked and warped. The cranial fragments include one piece of the left parietal, a small fragment of the occipital including the internal occipital protuberance, and three frontal fragments including the left supra-orbital margin. These fragments are probably from a single adult. The identifiable post-cranial fragments include both femora and the right tibia. These pieces were only lightly burned or smoked. The right femur was heavily charred at one place on the anterior surface. The bone was broken here and was burned inside the break. The circumference of the right femur suggests that this was a female. These bones may represent a few fragments excavated from an earlier burial by the inhabitants of Snodgrass when the floor for Structure 19 was dug. They could have been burned accidentally. It is unlikely that this was an intentional cremation.

Structure 45 Burial 1 (July 1971). Structure 45 intruded on a burial made previously. Most of the bone was apparently removed when a house pit for Structure 45 was dug. All that remained were a few poorly preserved fragments of the post-cranial skeleton of an adult. Artifacts found near the burial included a lump of gray-white clay, a 2 in. shell-tempered body sherd, a small hammerstone (?) fragment, and a three-lobed concretion.

SNODGRASS SITE INFANT BURIALS

Burials 5 and 6, which should have been numbered according to the structures under which they were buried, were not the only infant burials found beneath the house floors at Snodgrass. Nine other clusters of bone identified as baby burials were examined in the lab. One turned out to be an adult (STR 45 B-1) and another turned out to be a turtle carapace (STR 51 B-1). Six of the other seven could be aged by the development of the occipital bone (Redfield 1970) and were all under three months in age. The infant in B-1 from STR 48 could not be aged because the occipital was not recovered.

Structure 42 Burial 1. This infant was represented by some crumbling long bones, the petrous parts of the temporals, the basi-occipital bones, and a few fragments of the cranial vault. Two large jar sherds, one from the rim and one from the body, were associated with the burial. Also found in the fill were pieces of shell and charcoal.

Structure 42 Burial 2. The remains of this infant included a few ribs and vertebrae, the petrous portion of both temporals, the basi-occipital bones, large fragments of the vault, and part of the crown of a deciduous molar. A large bowl rim and a large body sherd were found with the infant. Two flint chips in the burial may have been part of the fill.

Structure 44 Burial 1. The fragmentary post-cranial bones of this infant included both femora, both humeri, both tibiae, and the right scapula. The ribs and vertebrae were also well represented. The cranial material included the mandible and a few tooth crowns, the petrous temporals, both supra-orbital margins, and a few vault fragments. A miniature human effigy bowl was placed at the infant's head.

Structure 47 Burial 1. Both ilia, both femora, and a few ribs of an infant were represented by fragments. Both temporals were also recovered, along with the basi-occipital, some vault fragments, and the left half of the mandible. A tiny jar made from the hollow leg of a larger vessel was found with the burial. A fragment of a deer molar may have been part of the fill.

Structure 48 Burial 1. (382S/823E). An infant was represented by post-cranial bones which included the left ulna and radius and a few metacarpals. The cranium was represented by the petrous parts of both temporals, a single vault fragment, and fragments of the left and right partes laterales of the occipital. Associated with the burial was a large elliptical sherd cut from a jar.

Structure 50 Burial 1. The only post-cranial bones of the infant that could be salvaged were the right femur and two vertebral arches. The left half of the mandible was recovered with both incisors. The basi-occipital and both inner ears were also recovered. The chert fragment and two small sherds found with the burial may have been pit fill.

Structure 77 Burial 1 (149S/1031E). The only bones of this infant that were recovered were the basi-occipital bones, both petrous temporals, the nuchal table of the occipital, and a few other vault fragments. A large, oblong body sherd from a jar was included in the burial.

The Powers Fort Burials

The Powers Fort burials were removed during several salvage operations. There is no provenience for most of them and they are widely separated. It is not known whether they came from a cemetery.

Burial 1 (September 1964). A 30-year-old male was extended with his head to the west-northwest, facing up. His sex was determined from pelvic and cranial form. This is an excellently preserved, rearticulated burial. Both femora have their anterior surfaces down, and the left tibia is reversed so that the distal end articulates with the distal end of the left femur. None of the long bones show cut marks such as might be made by a knife, but most of them are gnawed. However, the skull does show a number of cut marks which were probably made in order to remove the flesh when the body was prepared for burial. This man stood about 170 cm tall, had an undeformed skull, and may have died from a traumatic injury. The tip of a chert projectile point was lodged in the posterior surface of the left femur at the junction between the neck and the ball (Pl. 9). The compact bone in the area has broken away, so only the trabeculae may be examined for evidence of healing. The trabeculae are compressed next to the point tip and show no signs of reaction. The left acetabulum shows no signs of injury or change. Since this was a rearticulated burial, it is not certain that the point was introduced before B-1 died, although this is probably the case. Serial X-rays taken through the ball of the femur have added little information. B-1 could have been bending over at the waist or running when he was hit.

If all of the bones in the burial reached the lab, then when this individual was buried, the following bones were omitted: sternum, right clavicle, all but one rib, all cervical and seven thoracic vertebrae, both fibulae, both patellas, both hands, and both feet. He was buried with a long-necked water bottle placed about half a foot above his right shoulder.

Burial 2 (December 1964). Burial 2 was a 68-year-old male extended with his head to the south, facing up. His sex was determined from pelvic and cranial morphology. Preservation was excellent, but a few bones had been removed accidentally during plowing. His skull showed an intermediate degree of occipital flattening. He would have stood about 168 cm tall, if his arthitic condition did not interfere with a fully erect posture. The last four lumbar vertebrae were fused by osteophytes and may have been fused to the first lumbar vertebra and to the sacrum (Pl. 8). The thoracic and cervical vertebrae also showed varying degrees of lipping. The xiphoid process was fused to the body of the sternum which was in the process of fusing to the manubrium. The clavicles were nearly fused to the manubrium and the right first rib was fused to it. The joints of the hand showed some arthritic lipping and most of the other joints of the body showed small amounts of lipping. There is no evidence of eburnation at any of the joints. Many of his teeth were carious or had been lost through loosening by abscesses.

The artifacts buried with him included five Scallorn points (four around the head, one by the left arm); a bone fishhook under the mandible; four flint chips, a pebble hammerstone, an antler flaking tool, and two crystal artifacts by the left arm; a scraper by the right shoulder; and a water bottle on the left side of the cranium. A single child's metacarpal was mixed in with the bones of the left hand.

Burials 3 and 4 (April 1965). These are actually two individuals in one burial. Burial 3 is a 62-year-old male extended with his head to the west-northwest and facing north. Burial 4 is the bundle burial of an old male. He was placed between the legs of B-3 with his head on the west side of the bundle. Part of the bundle is to the right of the right humerus of B-3. B-4 will be renamed "B-3B" and B-3 will become "B-3A." Although the field notes refer to the preservation as poor, the bones located in the lab were in fine condition. The burials appeared fairly complete on the burial map, but the only post-cranial bone that could be located in the lab was the distal left femur of A. A turtle carapace (perhaps a knee rattle) was found at the distal end of the right femur of A. One projectile point was found near the foot of A. Both men had lost a few teeth before death. Neither skull showed any intentional deformation.

Burial 5 (April 1965). Burial 5 was an adult extended with its head to the east. The burial had been nearly completely destroyed by plowing, and none of the fragments were salvaged to be returned to the lab. The base of a pottery vessel destroyed by the plowing was found near the left shoulder.

Burial 6 (July 1969). This is an adult female extended with her head to the west. Her sex was determined from her femoral circumference. The bone was in fairly good condition, but had been disturbed by rodents. Most of the bones were present, but few of them could be located in the lab. She stood about 154 cm tall and had an undeformed skull.

A ring of osteitic bone circles her skull, running through the frontal, both parietals, and the top of the occipital (Pl. 10). In places the groove is wide, with islands of unaffected bone in the middle and with several holes eroded completely through the skull. A large chunk of bone is missing along the lambdoidal suture from lambda nearly to right asterion. The erosion clearly began exocranially. The groove is quite similar to the one Snow observed on the skull of a 24-year-old female from Moundville (Snow 1941b). That groove was thought to be the result of osteitis caused by a deep cut into the periosteum during scalping. If scalping was the cause of the injury to B-6, she evidently survived for quite some time before succumbing. Owsley and Berryman (1975) describe another similar case from the Middle Mississippian Arnold site in Williamson County, Tennessee. They state, however, that they would not definitely attribute the grooving of an adult male's skull to infection resulting from scalping. Hamperl (1967) and Morse (1969) both suggest that the Moundville specimen does not represent the results of scalping, unless it was an unsuccessful attempt, since the entire top of the vault should have been infected if the scalp were removed. Furthermore, post-mortem deterioration cannot be ruled out (Ubelaker 1978:75). Thus, the cause of the inflammation of the skull of B-6 is uncertain. No artifacts were buried with her.

POWERS FORT INFANT BURIALS

In July of 1969, a single structure was excavated at Powers Fort. Underneath Structure 1 were three baby burials.

Structure 1 Burial 1 (12.6N/17.0E). This was an infant aged under three months. It was in good condition; however, not all of its bones were represented in the lab.

Structure 1 Burial 2 (6.4N/6.9E). An infant aged three to six months was buried in a trash pit with its head to the north. Virtually all the bones were preserved, except the hands and feet.

Structure 1 Burial 3 (10.2N/7.0E). The third infant was under three months in age. It was nearly complete, but may have been disturbed by rodents. Associated objects included a large sherd placed under the head and a rodent jaw.

3

The Physical Analyses

Cranial Measurements and Cranial Deformation

Only 17 of the Powers phase crania could be restored sufficiently to permit measurements (Pls. 6 and 7). Three measurements were chosen to give an indication of size and shape: maximum cranial length (MAX CR L), maximum cranial breadth (MAX CR B), and maximum cranial height (MAX CR H). Two other measurements were added in order to test the applicability of a discriminant function for sexing Negroes that appeared in Giles (1970). These were maximum bizygomatic breadth (MAX BZ BR) and mastoid length (MAST L). The first four measurements were made with a spreading caliper following the method of Hooton (1946). The last was made with a sliding caliper following the method of Keen (1950). Measuring error with the spreading caliper is considered to be ±0.5 mm for the four measurements. Although the sliding caliper permits greater precision, the difficulty of properly orienting the instrument leads to an estimate of a measuring error of ±0.2 mm. In Table 2 the numbers enclosed in parentheses are estimates; these may be considered to have an error of ±3 mm.

Giles (1970) noted that discriminant functions calculated for one race to be used in sexing skeletal material frequently work for other races. As an extreme example, Giles and Elliot (1963) correctly sexed 89.4 percent of 85 adult chimpanzees using a discriminant function based on Whites and Negroes. Negro function 11 from Giles (1970) required only four measurements, all of which could be made or estimated for nine specimens from the Powers phase. These measurements were substituted into the equation

$$N = 2.11(MAX\ CR\ L)+(MAX\ CR\ B)+4.963(MAX\ BZ\ BR)+8.037(MAST\ L)$$

and the resulting values of N were compared to the section point of 1387.72. All skulls with values exceeding this number were considered male; all others were considered female. The results of the application of the discriminant

TABLE 2 Cranial Measurements
(Figures in Parentheses are Estimates.)

Site	*Individual*	*Sex*	*Deformation*	*MAX CR L*	*MAX CR B*	*MAX CR H*	*MAX BZ BR*	*MAST L*	*CI*
Turner	6A	I	none	(171)	-	(138)	-	-	-
Turner	7	F	slight	(161)	149.0	-	(125)	20.5	92.5
Turner	13C	F	none	170.5	125.0	140.5	126.5	25.6	73.3
Turner	17A	F	by soil	165.0	133.0	(134)	-	-	80.6
Turner	20	M	heavy	154.0	165.0	(140)	-	-	107.1
Turner	25A	F	none	(176)	-	-	-	-	-
Turner	33B	M	none	(180)	-	-	-	-	-
Turner	47	F	intermediate	(154)	153.0	-	-	-	-
Turner	51	M	none	174.5	(146)	-	-	-	-
Turner	61 CF-2	F	none	162.5	(139)	-	(129)	22.9	85.5
Turner	unassigned calvarium	M	intermediate	162.0	142.0	-	-	-	87.6
Snodgrass	3	F	by soil	(150)	(141)	-	(128)	26.2	-
Snodgrass	4A	M	intermediate	(159)	(142)	145.0	(137)	26.8	81.4
Powers Fort	1	M	none	(170)	146.0	138.5	(137)	32.8	85.9
Powers Fort	2	M	intermediate	(177)	145.0	(142)	(144)	30.3	81.9
Powers Fort	3A	M	none	177.0	145.0	(142)	(144)	30.3	81.9
Powers Fort	3B	M	none	(177)	(144)	-	(147)	28	81.4

function are listed in Table 3, along with the sex of the individuals as previously determined by inspection. Only one of the nine crania was misclassified, and this was a deformed male skull with four estimated measurements (4A from Snodgrass).

The Negro discriminant function performed well on this sample of Native Americans and gave virtually the same results as sexing by visual inspection. This is very encouraging, since some of these measurements can be made or estimated on fragmentary skulls before they are removed from the ground and have the opportunity to disintegrate. In particular, the bizygomatic breadth of the Turner skulls could have been measured when the skulls were in the ground, since the malars were often preserved and still in place. However, because the main part of the face was usually decomposed, when a cranium was removed from the ground, the face could no longer be restored and the bizygomatic breadth was lost.

Sexing by cranial discriminant functions and sexing by the midshaft circumference of the femur are two useful techniques for sexing poorly preserved skeletal material in the field. If these techniques had been employed at the time of excavation, more individuals could have been sexed, and more would be known about those remains which have been lost or misidentified since excavation.

The Cranial Index

$$CI = MAX\ CR\ BR/MAX\ CR\ L \times 100$$

was calculated for all skulls for which both measurements were made, regardless of deformation (Table 3). The deformed skulls may be quickly recognized by their generally high values for the index. The other skulls may be classified by their CI values as follows: dolichocranic (CI < 75.00), one; mesocranic

TABLE 3 Discriminant Function Sexing of Crania

Site	*Individual*	*Deformation*	*N*	*Discriminant Function Sex*	*Previously Determined Sex*
Turner	7	yes	1301.22	F	F
Turner	13C	no	1318.49	F	F
Turner	61 CF-2	no	1306.31	F	F
Snodgrass	3	by soil	1303.48	F	F
Snodgrass	4A	yes	1375.97	F	M
Powers Fort	1	no	1448.41	M	M
Powers Fort	2	yes	1474.77	M	M
Powers Fort	3	no	1476.84	M	M
Powers Fort	4	no	1472.24	M	M

(75.00 ⩽ CI < 80.00), none; brachycranic (80.00 ⩽ CI < 85.00), four; hyper-brachycranic (85.00 ⩽ CI), two. The skulls are short, wide, and high, with the exception of B-13C which is medium long, narrow, and high.

All Powers phase crania were examined for evidence of artificial deformation. The only type of intentional deformation discovered was occipital flattening. This varied in degree from slight, where only a small area near lambda was flattened, to intermediate, to heavy, where virtually the entire upper table of the occipital had been flattened. A total of 33 individuals was examined; 24 from Turner, 4 from Snodgrass, and 5 from Powers Fort. The results for each site are listed, along with the sex of the individuals, in Table 4.

The only heavily deformed crania were three males and one individual of indeterminate sex from Turner. Sample size is not large enough to permit the testing of the hypothesis that among the deformed skulls, the males were more heavily deformed. However, a four-fold table may be composed for all three sites to test whether either sex has deformed crania significantly more often than the other. Nine males and eight females had undeformed crania, and eight males and four females had crania deformed to varying degrees. The The probable cause of the deformation is the binding of the infant's head to a cradleboard. The Luxembourg memoir, cited in Swanton (1911:54), describes the method of cranial deformation employed by the early historic

TABLE 4 Artificial Deformation of Crania

Site	*Indiv.*	*Sex**	*Deformation*#	*Site*	*Indiv.*	*Sex*	*Deformation*
Turner	6A	I	0	Turner	40	F	S
Turner	7	F	S	Turner	47	F	I
Turner	8A	I	H	Turner	51	M	0
Turner	13C	F	0	Turner	54 CF-1	M	I
Turner	15	F	0	Turner	60	M	0
Turner	16A	M	0	Turner	61 CF-2	F	0
Turner	20	M	H	Turner	unassigned calvarium	M	I
Turner	21A	M	0				
Turner	22A	M	H	Snodgrass	1 CF-1	I	S
Turner	23	M	I	Snodgrass	3	F	0
Turner	25A	F	0	Snodgrass	4A	M	I
Turner	27	F	I	Snodgrass	7	F	0
Turner	33A	M	I	Powers Fort	1	M	0
Turner	33B	M	0	Powers Fort	2	M	I
Turner	33C	J	H	Powers Fort	3A	M	0
Turner	36B	F	0	Powers Fort	3B	M	0
Turner	38E	F	0	Powers Fort	6	F	0

*M = male, F = female, J = juvenile, I = indeterminate
#0 = none, S = slight, I = intermediate, H = heavy

Natchez. An infant's head was bound between two boards every night and it slept this way until its skull had taken on the desired shape.

POPULATION RELATIONSHIPS OF THE POWERS PHASE

The biological relationships among prehistoric populations have long been of interest to physical anthropologists and archaeologists. The studies of populational affinities often involve the compilation of huge lists of skeletal measurements and traits and their comparison with multivariate statistics. In fact, many of the multivariate statistics now in general use were originally developed to deal with the comparisons of skeletal populations.

In recent years, several studies of prehistoric population relationships have sought to compare measures of biological distance based on skeletal measurements with measures of biological distance based on discrete traits (Rightmire 1972; Corruccini 1974). Little can be contributed here to the debate about the relative merits of the two different kinds of distances, because too few Powers phase crania could be measured to compute any sort of biological distance on the basis of craniometrics. However, discrete (present or absent) traits of the cranium could be recorded for many of the Powers phase crania, so that it is possible to examine the biological distances, as reflected in the discrete traits, between the Powers phase and other selected populations. It should be noted that the "biological distances" based on discrete traits may not correspond to the distances which could be computed were actual genealogies available. It has been assumed by many authors that the discrete traits are primarily genetic in character, but the actual genetics of most of the traits are at best poorly understood.

It would be of particular interest to compare the Powers phase population to other Mississippian populations, particularly populations from nearby regions, and to earlier populations in the same area. Published nonmetric data on skeletal populations from the region of southeast Missouri are few, so that only very limited comparisons may be made.

A total of 39 discrete skeletal traits were recorded for the Powers phase crania, but many could be scored for only a few individuals. Sixteen of the traits (Table 5) could be recorded for ten or more individuals, and their frequencies appear in Table 6 (these traits are defined and illustrated in Berry and Berry 1967; Birkby 1973; and McWilliams 1974). Also tabulated in Table 6 are trait frequencies for three other Mississippian populations and one Southwestern population. Data for the three Mississippian populations, Hazel and Vernon Paul in Arkansas, and Kane in Illinois, were made available by Dr. David J. Wolf of the University of Kentucky. Trait frequencies for the Grasshopper population from Arizona were taken from Birkby (1973). Only adults are used, and sexes are pooled for all groups.

TABLE 5 Discrete Traits Recorded for Powers Phase Crania

1. Auditory torus
2. Ossicle at lambda
3. Ossicle in lambdoid suture
4. *Os Inca*
5. Ossicle at asterion
6. Parietal notch bone
7. Zygo-facial foramen present
8. Parietal foramen present
9. Mastoid foramen present
10. Posterior condylar canal patent
11. Hypoglossal canal double
12. Tympanic dehiscence
13. Mental foramen double
14. Metopic suture
15. Mylo-hyoid bridge
16. Ossicle in coronal suture

TABLE 6 Observations on Discrete Traits*

Trait	*Powers Phase*		*Hazel*		*Upper Nodena*		*Kane*		*Grasshopper*	
	n‡	*k*#	*n*	*k*	*n*	*k*	*n*	*k*	*n*	*k*
1.	52	3	50	33	56	32	58	3	161	0
2.	23	10	35	16	48	21	43	13	130	32
3.	27	21	50	25	53	44	52	39	137	70
4.	32	0	44	2	54	1	54	2	160	1
5.	30	13	42	35	45	28	44	32	152	41
6.	35	6	43	13	49	4	34	11	156	17
7.	14	11	40	37	48	40	35	23	155	149
8.	29	16	51	35	57	13	59	28	153	124
9.	24	22	45	42	53	41	43	37	159	152
10.	13	10	32	29	42	34	31	26	138	136
11.	27	6	36	6	42	22	25	8	149	38
12.	46	3	48	37	45	32	48	17	161	45
13.	39	4	87	6	41	3	48	4	155	12
14.	42	0	52	0	57	1	67	3	159	1
15.	34	2	74	13	42	6	42	4	149	26
16.	14	0	44	22	51	10	46	7	132	2

*Data for Hazel, Upper Nodena, and Kane courtesy of Dr. David J. Wolf of the University of Kentucky. Data for Grasshopper from Birkby (1973).
n‡ = the number of times a trait could be observed to be present or absent.
k# = the number of times a trait was observed to be present.

The statistic most trequently used to compute a biological distance from discrete traits is the Mean Measure of Divergence (MMD). The trait frequencies are first converted to angular measure, so that the variance is independent of the trait frequencies. The recommended transformation is the Freeman-Tukey inverse sine transformation:

$$\theta = [\sin^{-1}\{1\text{-}2k/(n+1)\} + \sin^{-1}\{1\text{-}2(k+1)/(n+1)\}]/2;$$

where k is the observed number of presences of a trait, n is the number of times the trait may be observed to be present or absent, and θ is measured in radians and has a variance of approximately $1/(n+½)$ (Freeman and Tukey 1950; Green and Suchey 1976).

The MMD may then be computed as:

$$MMD = \Sigma\, [\theta_{1i} - \theta_{2i}]^2 - \{1/(n_{1i} + ½) + 1/(n_{2i} + ½)\}\ ]/r;$$

where r is the number of traits considered, θ_{1i} and θ_{2i} are the transformed frequencies of the ith trait in the first and second populations, and n_{1i} and n_{2i} are the number of crania in the first and second populations examined for trait i (Green and Suchey 1976).

The variance of the MMD is computed as:

$$V = (2/r^2) \times \Sigma[1/(n_{1i} + ½) + 1/(n_{2i} + ½)]^2;$$

(Sjovold 1973). The variance may be used to test the MMD for significance. If the MMD is more than twice the square root of the variance, then the null hypothesis (of no difference between the populations) may be rejected. The test is significant at about $p = 0.03$ (Green and Suchey 1976).

The results of the computation of the MMD and the standard deviations of the MMD for the five populations are presented in Table 7. All the distances are significant. The nearest pair is Kane and the Powers phase, which might suggest some connection between the Powers phase and the Cahokia area. This interpretation is weakened by the second closest pairing, Grasshopper and the Powers phase. It is difficult to make sense of this result, which shows the Powers phase to be more closely related to a Southwestern population than to two Mississippian populations from nearby in Arkansas. Several explana-

TABLE 7 Mean Measures of Divergence (With Standard Deviations in Parentheses) Among Five Skeletal Populations*

	Hazel	*Upper Nodena*	*Kane*	*Grasshopper*
Powers Phase	.43027 (.02236)	.25021 (.02165)	.10355 (.02282)	.11601 (.01699)
Hazel		.13157 (.01505)	.25096 (.01601)	.48690 (.01020)
Upper Nodena			.14829 (.01564)	.41371 (.00963)
Kane				.20897 (.01032)

*Distances are significant at the $p = .03$ level of probability if they are equal to or greater than twice their standard deviations. Distance computations are based on sixteen traits. All distances are significant.

tions are possible for this situation. First, it could be argued that Wolf scored traits differently than Birkby or the author. However, Wolf's three populations do not form a tight cluster; Kane is more similar to Grasshopper than to Hazel. Second, the use of a short trait list may have caused misleading results; that is, one or two very divergent traits (the auditory torus, for example) could have given rise to the differences. However, it would be contrary to the usual pattern, in which distances become increasingly significant as the trait list lengthens, if for no other reason than that the variance decreases as the inverse of the number of traits (Sjovold 1973; Black 1979). Third, it is possible that the MMD is more suited to differentiating closely related populations than more distantly related groups. This explanation seems unlikely, since the MMD has been utilized with a fair amount of success (and with some "incorrect" results) for differentiating populations from around the world (Berry and Berry 1967). The fourth explanation for the unexpected results on the MMD is that the discrete traits utilized here are not primarily genetic, but also include "noise" from environmental and physiological sources. This explanation is preferred to the other three.

The results of this brief study of population relationships have shed little light on the "position" of the Powers phase population among the prehistoric cultures of the southeastern United States. Perhaps when more is known of the genetics of discrete traits, the list of tabulated data for the Powers phase may prove useful to other students.

Stature

In recent years, several studies have been completed which enable the osteologist to get a much better and more complete idea of the stature of the individuals represented in a skeletal population. Genovés (Genovés 1967; Bass 1971) used a sample of Middle American Indians to develop regression formulae predicting stature from the lengths of the femur, the tibia, and the combined long bones. Another set of regression equations provided by Trotter and Gleser (1958) would permit calculation of stature from the humerus as well as the femur and tibia. However, the standard deviations of their estimates were larger than Genovés's and the number of measurable humeri from the Powers phase was small. For these reasons, Genovés's formulae were chosen for the estimation of the stature of the Powers phase people.

Relatively few individuals from the Powers phase sites have completely restorable long bones. However, Steele and McKern (1969) published a series of regression formulae for predicting long bone length from the lengths of certain segments of the bones. They defined six measuring points on the tibia and humerus and five on the femur (Fig. 5). They then measured the parallel length of each bone and the length of each segment and of all combinations of adjacent segments for 117 Middle Mississippian Indians from northeast Arkansas. The segment lengths expressed as percentages of the total length of each bone from the lengths of its segments were then computed for each sex and for the combined sample. It seemed likely that these equations would be excellent predictors of long bone length for the Powers phase Mississippians.

The segment lengths of every complete and fragmentary femur and tibia from the Powers phase were measured following Steele and McKern's methods, then analyzed. Too few complete long bones were found to permit calculation of Powers phase regression formulae; but enough femora were available to test the applicability of Steele and McKern's formulae. Since there were only six test cases for males and seven for females, no more than one failure of prediction was considered permissible for any formula. In other words, a formula which incorrectly predicted the length of more than one of the intact femora was unacceptable. In general, the regression equations for combined bone segments were much better predictors than the equations for single segments. The only formulae which met the criterion of acceptability were the multiple regressions based on Segments 1 and 2 and Segments 2 and 3 for males and females. Actual femur length was always within ±2 standard deviations of the predictions, with the single exception of B-33A to the equation for Segments 1 and 2 for the males. The other regression formulae for combined segments had too many misses to be acceptable.

Several sources of error may be involved in the inadequacy of most of the equations. First of all, it is no simple matter to identify all of Steele and McKern's landmark points. For example, point 4 on the tibia is located "where the anterior crest of the tibia . . . crosses to the mid-section of the shaft" (Steele and McKern 1969:217). The placement of this point is dependent on how the observer orients the shaft. This is not too great a difficulty with a complete tibia, but it becomes a real problem when only the shaft is available. Although this point was the most difficult to locate, it was by no means the only problem point. Thus, the points of measurement may have been incorrectly identified on the Powers phase bones. All points were marked on the bones in pencil, so if another researcher is interested in investigating this problem, he will be able to compare his own measuring points to those used in this study.

A second source of error relates to the reproducibility of measurements. This is not a major difficulty here. Six intact bones (two femora, two tibiae,

---

*Explanation of figure quoted from Steele and McKern (1969: 226).
Figure redrawn after Steele and McKern (1969: 227, Pl. 1).

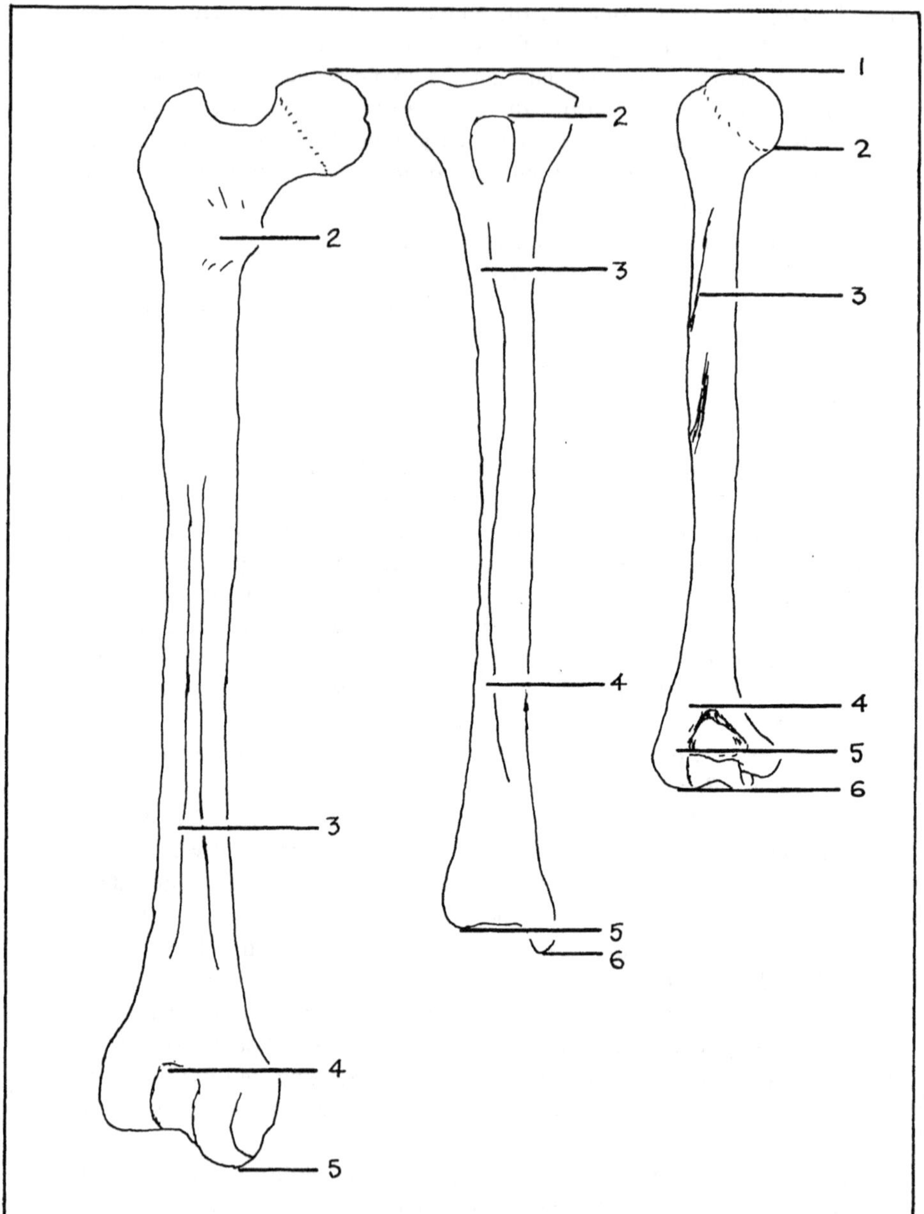

Figure 5. Landmarks of Long Bones

FIGURE 5 EXPLANATION OF FIGURE

On the femur, the landmarks demarcating the sections of the bone are (1) the most proximal point of the long bone; (2) the midpoint of the lesser trochanter; (3) the anterior point of the popliteal surface; (4) the proximal border of the intercondylar fossa; (5) the distal point of the bone.

The landmarks used for demarcation of the sections of the tibia are (1) the most proximal point of the tibia; (2) the most proximal point of the tibial tuberosity; (3) the point of confluence of the lines from the lower end of the tuberosity; (4) the point where the anterior crest of the tibia crosses over the medial border of the shaft above the medial malleolus; (5) the proximal margin of the inferior articular facet; (6) the distal point of the medial malleolus.

On the humerus the lines of demarcation are (1) the most proximal point of the head; (2) the most distal point of the circumference of the head; (3) the point of narrowest diameter anteriorly/posteriorly when measured proximally to the deltoid tuberosity; (4) the proximal margin of the olecranon fossa; (5) the distal margin of the olecranon fossa; (6) the distal point of the trochlea.

two humeri) were set aside and measured every day before any Powers phase bones were measured. The average measurement error during the four trials on the standards was less than one percent.

The third source of error is the possibility that the mixed Middle Mississippian sample from northeast Arkansas was sufficiently different genetically from the southeast Missouri population that it is unreasonable to expect the regression equations to work. This would be very unfortunate, since no regression equations can be derived for the Powers phase using Steele and McKern's method. In addition, this would mean that Genovés's formulae are probably inapplicable, too. This unhappy thought can be ignored for the time being, since there is a much more important reason for the deficiency of the regression equations.

The fourth, and most important, source of error is intrinsic to Steele and McKern's formulae. It is not possible to recompute new formulae from their data, since they are not presented, but several of their tables may be tested against each other. Taking three arbitrary femur lengths—40 cm, 45 cm and 50 cm—the expected lengths of each femur segment may be generated using the formulae in their Table 7 (see my Table 8, columns B and C). Using Genovés's formulae, it can be shown that femora of these lengths would belong to males with statures of 156.8 cm (61.7 in.), 168.1 cm (66.2 in.), and 179.4 cm (70.6 in.), respectively. None of these is an unreasonable stature for an American Indian (cf. average stature of males among different Plains Indian groups in Wissler [1920]). Using the regression formulae for male femora published in Steele and McKern's Table 10 (1969), the expected

TABLE 8 A Test of Steele and McKern's (1969) Regression Formulae for Predicting Femur Length

A	B	C			D		
Segment Combination	*Male Mean %*	*Expected Segment Length*			*Predicted Femur Length*		
		40 cm	*45 cm*	*50 cm*	*40 cm*	*45 cm*	*50 cm*
1	16.4	6.6	7.4	8.2	43.6	44.8	46.1
2	56.1	22.4	25.2	28.0	41.9	43.8	45.8
3	19.4	7.8	8.7	9.7	44.5	44.8	45.1
4	7.9	3.2	3.6	4.0	44.2	45.0	45.8
1-2	72.5				42.0	44.6	47.3
2-3	75.5				41.3	45.7	50.2
3-4	27.3				43.8	44.9	46.1
1-3	91.9				38.8	43.4	48.1
2-4	83.5				39.5	44.0	48.7

length of each femur can be calculated from each of its segment lengths (Table 8, column D). An error was made in the regression formulae as published in Tables 10, 11, and 12 in Steele and McKern (1969). The multipliers for all the segment lengths are too small by a factor of ten. This error has been corrected for the femora in Table 9, and the corrected formulae for the males are used in calculating the figures in column D of Table 8.

The results shown in Table 8 are disturbing. All of the single segment formulae over-estimate the length of the short femur and underestimate the length of the long femur, although most of the multiple segment formulae are fairly accurate. Thus, there is a tendency for the single segment equations to reduce the apparent variability of stature of any population under study. If the regression formulae are used only on fragmentary bones, while the intact bones are measured only for total length, the effect is to create two distinct sub-populations. They may share the same mean, but one group will be much more variable than the other. The incautious observer may then begin to form hypotheses based on a non-existent difference. At the very least, the number of individuals with extreme stature will be reduced.

Because few of the regression formulae did an adequate job, another approach was tried. It was decided to test the predictive power of the percentage lengths of the femora and tibiae for bone length. Three figures were generated from each segment length as follows. The mean percentage figures for males, females, and combined sex were divided into their respective segment lengths to give a median figure. Then the mean percentage plus two standard deviations were divided into the appropriate segment length to give a "short" bone length. Finally, a "long" bone length was calculated by dividing the segment length by the mean percentage less two standard devia-

TABLE 9 Corrected Regression Formulae for Predicting Femur Length*

Segments	*Male*
1	32.94+1.6(S1)#=femur±1.39 cm
2	26.20+0.7(S2)=femur±1.31 cm
3	42.18+0.3(S3)=femur±1.67 cm
4	37.44+2.1(S4)=femur±1.56 cm
1-2	20.63+1.2(S1)+0.6(S2)=femur±1.09 cm
2-3	5.89+1.2(S2)+1.1(S3)=femur±0.75 cm
3-4	34.77+0.3(S3)+2.1(S4)=femur±1.52 cm
1-3	1.36+1.1(S1)+1.0(S2)+1.0(S3)=femur±0.33 cm
2-4	2.158+1.1(S2)+1.0(S3)+1.4(S4)=femur±0.58 cm
Segments	*Female*
1	36.55+0.8(S1)=femur±1.23 cm
2	28.46+0.6(S2)=femur±1.02 cm
3	38.90+0.3(S3)=femur±1.23 cm
4	37.98+1.1(S4)=femur±1.24 cm
1-2	17.99+1.3(S1)+0.7(S2)=femur±0.86 cm
2-3	10.52+1.0(S2)+1.0(S3)=femur±0.51 cm
3-4	32.45+0.5(S3)+1.6(S4)=femur±1.52 cm
1-3	3.64+1.0(S1)+1.0(S2)+0.9(S3)=femur±0.28 cm
2-4	7.53+0.9(S2)+1.1(S3)+1.0(S4)=femur±0.44 cm

*Modified from Steele and McKern (1969: Table 10).
#The numbers in parentheses, preceded by the letter "S," designate the section.

tions. The results were checked for all femora where total length was known. A number of predictors were ruled out because they gave too wide a range. Others failed to include the true bone length within their range. The final group of predictors was characterized by having narrow ranges and including all or most of the femora of known length within their ranges. There was little difference between the male, female, and neuter formulae, so, for convenience, only the neuter set was used. The acceptable predictors for femora were based on four combinations of femoral segments and length ranges. The first combination was that of sequences 1 and 2, used over the range of median to long. The second combination was that of segments 2 and 3, used over the range of short to long. The third combination was that of segments 1, 2, and 3, used over the range of short to median. The fourth combination was that of segments 2, 3, and 4, used over the range of short to long. The only good predictor of tibia length was the combination of segments 1, 2, 3, and 4, used over the range of median to long. All of these had narrow ranges, generally 25 mm or less, and all performed well as predictors on bones of known length.

Stature was calculated for 16 individuals with complete long bones, using Genovés's formulae as corrected in Bass (1971) (Table 10). Some of the long bone lengths were augmented by small amounts to compensate for damaged epiphyses. Stature could be estimated for another 21 individuals using long bone lengths predicted from measurements of segment lengths. The statures of these individuals are best represented as ranges, but only a figure representing the central tendency is presented in Table 11. Where more than one estimate of a bone's length was possible, the different estimates were examined for areas of overlap. When several estimates did overlap, the range of the bone length was narrowed to the area of overlap, and the midpoint of this range was used to calculate stature. A few individuals had several nonoverlapping estimates of bone length and were excluded from the sample.

TABLE 10 Regression Formulae for Predicting Stature from Long Bone Length*

Male
2.26(femur)+663.79=stature±34.17
1.96(tibia)+937.52=stature±28.15
Female
2.59(femur)+497.42=stature±38.16
2.72(tibia)+637.81=stature±35.13

*From Bass (1971: Table 9).

None of the stature estimates has been corrected for the loss in height said to occur with increasing age (Trotter and Gleser 1952). These statures are actually skeletal lengths; to get the true height of the living individual, subtract 2.5 cm (Genovés 1967).

Table 12 is a histogram comparing the distribution of stature by sex. A certain amount of overlap is apparent in the distributions, yet the sexual dimorphism is still clear. No female exceeds the mean male stature, and no male is smaller than the female mean. The distributions appear normal; however, because of the different methods used to estimate long bone length and stature, no tests of normality were made, and no standard deviations were calculated.

The average stature of the Powers phase Indians is compared to that of other Mississippian and related groups in Table 13. The stature figures given for the other sites, except Dickson Mounds, are not the ones presented in the original reports, since they were calculated using Pearson's (1899) or Trotter

TABLE 11 Individual Statures*

Site	*Individual*	*Sex*	*Stature (cm)*	*Site*	*Individual*	*Sex*	*Stature (cm)*
23BU21B	3	F	166*	23BU21A	25A	F	151
23BU21B	7	F	160	23BU21A	26	M	164
23BU10	1	M	170*	23BU21A	33A	M	174*
23BU10	2	M	168*	23BU21A	33B	M	169
23BU10	6	F	154*	23BU21A	35A	F	155
23BU21A	4	I	162 if F	23BU21A	35B	F	153
			164 if M	23BU21A	36A	M	172*
23BU21A	5A	M	164*	23BU21A	36B	F	152
23BU21A	6 F-1&8	F	153	23BU21A	47	F	162*
23BU21A	12A	F	168	23BU21A	48	F	152
23BU21A	13B	F	158*	23BU21A	49	F	155
23BU21A	13D or E	M	166*	23BU21A	52 F-1&6	M	174
23BU21A	15	F	163*	23BU21A	52 F-3	F	153
23BU21A	18A	F	151	23BU21A	52 F-4&5	M	164
23BU21A	20	M	173*	23BU21A	60	M	168*
23BU21A	22A	M	172	23BU21A	61 F-1&10	F	158
23BU21A	23	M	170	23BU21A	61 F-2&11	M	160
23BU21A	24A	M	166*	23BU21A	61 F-5&8	F	153
23BU21A	24C or D	F	164*	23BU21A	61 F-6&9	F	156

*These figures represent the central tendency of a range for each individual. A range of ±5 cm will most likely contain the true stature of the individual. Figures with an asterik next to them were calculated from complete long bones.

TABLE 12 Stature Histogram

Stature (cm)	*Female*	*Indeterminate*	*Male*
148 - 152	XXXX		
153 - 157	XXXXXXXX		
158 - 162	XXXX		X
163 - 167	XXX	X	XXXXX
168 - 172	X		XXXXXXX
173 - 177			XXX

Female Mean (N = 20):156.8 cm
Male Mean (N = 16):168.3 cm

and Gleser's (1958) formulae. Instead, the original data were used to calculate statures with Genovés's (1967) formulae. No data on femur length were available for Dickson Mounds, so stature was not recomputed. For three of the sites (Campbell, Moundville, and Steed-Kisker), the individual femur measure-

TABLE 13 Estimated Stature for Some Mississippian Populations

Site	*Method**	*Male Sample Size*	*Mean Male Stature (cm)*	*Female Sample Size*	*Mean Female Stature (cm)*
Powers Phase	I	16	168	20	157
Moundville (Snow 1941a)	I	9	167	7	159
Koger's Island (Newman and Snow 1942)	A	29	168	17	157
Steed-Kisker (Stewart 1943)	I	8	169	5	161
Madisonville (Hooton 1920)	A	29	168	19	158
Dickson Mounds (Harn 1971)	P	41	168	37	157
Campbell (Spier 1955)	I	13	169	7	158

*Key to methods used in estimating stature:
I = Individual statures computed, then averaged
A = Femur lengths averaged, then average stature computed
P = Individual statures computed by Pearson's method, raw data not available for recomputation

ments were available. In these cases, stature for an individual was determined from the longer femur or from the most accurately measured femur. The Koger's Island and Madisonville stature estimates were based on the longer of the left and right mean femur lengths. Thus, they are not strictly comparable with the others. The difference, however, is minimal, as can be seen from the Moundville male data. When stature for this sample was calculated from mean femur length, the results were 166 cm (right) and 168 cm (left). The number derived by averaging the estimates of individual maximum statures is 167 cm. The discrepancy is small enough that it should not affect the comparison.

There is nothing exceptional about the average stature of either sex in the Powers phase. The males fall in the middle of the Mississippian range, while the females are at the low end.

It has recently become the vogue to incorporate analyses of stature into investigations of nutrition and social organization (Buikstra 1972; Hatch and Willey 1974). The information on stature generated for the Powers phase population is obviously inadequate for such a study, especially considering the magnitude of the estimated errors involved. This raises the question, though, of the adequacy of the previous studies. That is, how accurately can stature be estimated, and how small a difference should be considered socially or nutritionally significant? Hatch and Willey ignored these problems when they accepted Madeline Kneberg's stature estimates with the statement that "technical errors, if any, are probably consistent throughout the sample" (1974: 110).

Stature calculated from skeletal remains is only an estimate, and as such, has an associated error of estimate. Stature is probably best considered as a range, rather than an absolute figure. For instance, Genoves's best regression formulae have an error figure of ±26 mm for males and ±28 mm for females, or about ±1 in. for each sex (Genovés 1967; Bass 1971). Very few of the stature differences among the groups analyzed by Hatch and Willey exceed two in. In view of this fact, their conclusions should be accepted only tentatively, since their significant differences may not be significant at all. Either a statistic which deals with data expressed as intervals should be used, or a different measure should be tested.

The length of one of the long bones could be substituted for stature, since the lengths of all the long bones are correlated with stature. An intact long bone can be measured fairly accurately, so the only error of concern is the reproducibility of the measurement. By rephrasing the original hypothesis, long bone length may then be tested, rather than stature. This approach has the added advantage of allowing one to use information from a variety of published sources, since methods of measuring long bones have been more uniform than means of calculating stature.

Pathology and Trauma

The study of pathology and trauma has been used to provide information regarding the general health of populations. More recently, Buikstra (1976, 1977a, 1977b) and Robbins (1971) have considered the interaction between disease processes and the nature of a population's adaptation to its environment. Although pathology and trauma are potentially valuable sources of information on the Powers phase population, the poor preservation and uneven recovery of skeletal material make it unreasonable to do more than document the observed pathological specimens.

A number of bones which appeared pathological were taken together with their X-rays to specialists familiar with bone pathologies and X-rays at the University of Michigan hospitals. Dr. William Martel was consulted about one specimen and Dr. Andrew Poznanski was consulted about three others.

A total of 14 individuals showing pathological and/or traumatic changes to the skeleton was recovered from Powers phase sites, 11 from Turner and three from Powers Fort. Six individuals had pathological changes to the skeleton, six had traumatic changes, and two had both.

Five of the seven pathologies involved bony changes related to arthritis. Individual B-2 from Powers Fort, a 68-year-old male, showed the most extensive arthritic changes to the skeleton. Virtually every joint surface showed some osteoarthritic lipping, and all of the vertebrae had osteophytic lipping, including the second through fifth lumbar vertebrae which were fused together (Pl. 8). The clavicles, right first rib, and sternum were in the process of fusing together. This fusion would have made respiration painful and difficult. The arthritic changes are listed in greater detail in Chapter 2.

B-60, an old male from Turner, had osteoarthritic lipping on the odontoid facet of the atlas. No other skeletal changes related to arthritis were observed, but poor preservation of the skeleton left few articular surfaces sufficiently intact for observation.

At least one of the females from B-18 at Turner had osteophytic lipping of some of the vertebrae, but it is uncertain which of the four women was affected.

Osteophytic lipping of some thoracic vertebrae was noted for B-35B from Turner, a 38-year-old female. No other arthritic changes were observed, but the skeleton was not completely preserved.

B-26, an adult male from Turner, had several compressed thoracic vertebrae which had osteophytic lipping. No other traumatic changes were observed on the incompletely preserved skeleton.

A single compressed thoracic vertebra with osteophytic lipping was recovered from B-55 at Turner. The vertebra is from one of the adults in the burial, but it is not known from which individual. An irregularly shaped tibia with an enlarged rectangular cross-section was also recovered from B-55. The tibia may be pathological. It was not clearly associated with any of the other skeletal material in the burial and could not be attributed to any particular individual.

The eighth pathology was a small smooth-walled pocket eroded in the diploe midway up the frontal of B-53B. The pocket would not have been discovered, except that the frontal was broken open at that point. Only one half of the bone containing the pocket was recovered. This was shown to Dr. Poznanski who suggested that the pocket represented an epidermoid cyst.

Two of the eight traumatic injuries, both compressed vertebrae, have been described with the pathologies. The remaining six are briefly described below.

Two femora from B-47, a 34-year-old female from Turner, had roughened surfaces which appeared to be the result of some periostitic inflammation. Dr. Martel suggested that this was due to an old trauma.

Two femora from B-41, an adult female from Turner, tapered unusually toward the distal end. The tapering occurred rather abruptly at midshaft, but amounted to no more than 1 cm in circumference. The surfaces of the bones were osteitic. These bones were shown to Dr. Poznanski who suggested that their appearance was the result of an old trauma.

Two tibiae, probably from one individual from B-61 at Turner, had somewhat irregular cross-sections and roughened surfaces. Dr. Poznanski could be no more specific than to suggest that their appearance was the result of an old trauma.

Two individuals were apparently wounded by arrows. A projectile point was recovered from the left innominate of B-31C, an adult male from Turner. The tip of a projectile point was found between the ball and neck of the left femur of B-1, a 30-year-old male from Powers Fort (Pl. 9). The posterior placement of both points suggests that the two men may have been bending over or running away from the persons who shot them. The injuries may have been the causes of death in each case. Both injuries were discussed in greater detail in Chapter 2.

B-6, an adult female from Powers Fort, exhibited a remarkable lesion on her skull (Pl. 10). A ring of osteitic bone circles her skull, running through the frontal, both parietals, and the top of the occipital. In places the groove is wide, with islands of unaffected bone in the middle and with several holes eroded completely through the skull. A large chunk of bone is missing along the lambdoidal suture from lambda nearly to right asterion. The erosion began exocranially. The groove is quite similar to the one Snow observed on the skull of a 24-year-old female from Moundville (Snow 1941b). That groove was thought to be the result of osteitis caused by a deep cut into the periosteum during scalping. If scalping was the cause of the injury to B-6, she evidently survived for quite some time before succumbing. Owsley and Berryman (1975) describe another, similar case from the Middle Mississippian Arnold site in Williamson County, Tennessee. They state, however, that they would not definitely attribute the grooving of an adult male's skull to infection resulting from scalping. Hamperl (1967) and Morse (1969) both suggest that the Moundville specimen does not represent the results of scalping, unless it is was unsuccessful attempt, since the entire top of the vault should have been infected if the scalp were removed. Furthermore, post-mortem deterioration cannot be ruled out (Ubelaker 1978: 75). Thus, the cause of the inflammation of the skull of B-6 is uncertain.

Even the limited data regarding pathologies and traumas presented above provides us with some information regarding the quality of life enjoyed by the Powers phase population.

It is evident that arthritis was a problem afflicting some of the adults, although it is not possible to estimate the percentage affected. The youngest case observed was just over thirty years of age. The oldest case was also the most severely afflicted—to the point where he must have been partly crippled and must have been at least partially reliant on the rest of the community for his well-being.

Three of the traumatic injuries provide evidence for prehistoric hostilities such as raiding and warfare. Two adult males were shot from behind with arrows. The nature of their injuries suggests that they were caught by surprise from behind or that they were fleeing from combat. One adult female may have been scalped, although the evidence is far from clear on this point. If she were scalped, then she survived for quite some time afterward. In some historic communities, the living victim of a scalping was exiled and forced to live alone (Gilmore 1934). Evidently, B-6 continued to participate in village life, since she was given a burial at Powers Fort. Whether her infirmity affected her status in the community is unknown, since too little is known about burials at Powers Fort for anything to be inferred from her place or mode of interment.

Dentition

Teeth are an ever-changing indicator of man's interaction with his environment. Inferences about food preparation, diet, and chewing habits may be made from observations of wear on teeth. Information concerning an individual's health during his childhood is recorded in the form of lines of enamel hypoplasia on the teeth. Although specific causes of the interruption of tooth growth may not be determined, the presence and frequency of the lines give a relative indication of the individual's health during the period of tooth formation. Oral disease is itself well-recorded in the forms of caries cavities, abscesses, periodontal disease, and lost teeth. The frequency and severity of dental disease should increase with age as the time of exposure to the risk of disease increases.

Teeth may also be used to investigate the biological relationships between populations. The number of cusps and the patterns of the grooves on the crowns of the molars are of interest in this respect. Although the form of the maxillary incisors is also of interest, too few incisors were retained in the jaws of the Powers phase skeletons for any kind of statistical treatment, and many of these were too worn for an assessment of the degree of shoveling. Suffice it to say that shoveled incisors were observed and seemed to be fairly common. Several interesting anomalies which are manifested in the dentition may also contain genetic information, but are not amenable to quantification because of the circumstances of discovery.

Artificial deformation of the teeth has been noted in a number of prehistoric populations (Romero 1958; Koritzer 1968; Ubelaker, Phenice, and Bass 1969; Wallace 1974), but was not observed on any of the Powers phase teeth.

Despite the fact that there were few complete dentitions among the skeletons recovered from the Powers phase sites, a good deal of information relevant to the topics mentioned above has been retrieved from the sample of teeth which was available.

CUSP PATTERNS

Cusp number and groove pattern were recorded only for adult molars still in the alveolus and for children's permanent molars which could be definitely assigned to a particular individual. Individuals over 15 years of age were considered to be adults. Cusp and fissure patterns of the lower molars were classified in the standard way (Bass 1971; Dahlberg 1951; Schuman and Brace 1955). In the *Y* pattern, the metaconid touches the hypoconid; in the + pattern, the protoconid touches the entoconid, or all four cusps touch. Dahlberg (1951:165) suggested the following system of recording the cusps of the maxillary molars: "4 designates four well developed cusps; 4- indicates a reduction in the size of the hypocone; 3+ indicates the absence of the hypocone, but the presence of a cuspule on the distal border; 3 indicates total absence of the hypocone." In practice, difficulty was experienced in distinguishing between the 4- and the 3+ states because of wear on the occlusal surfaces of the teeth. Since the original distinction seemed arbitrary and subjective, the class 3+ was modified to include the range from cuspule to reduced hypocone. Another class, 2+ was added to cover the situation when the metacone was greatly reduced and the hypocone was absent. Third molars were most variable in form and frequently had to be classified as "irregular."

The adult sample included 24 mandibles represented by 19 left sides and 20 right sides, and 22 maxillae represented by 20 left sides and 17 right sides. The predominant mandibular patterns were: first molar, Y5(94%); second molar, +5(76%); third molar, +5(39%) and irregular (25%) (Table 14). These frequencies are similar to those for other North American Indian groups as reported by Dahlberg (1951:155-57). As might be expected, the most common combination of patterns for the first two mandibular molars was *Y*5, +5 (72 percent of the mandible halves with both teeth). In the sample of children, 59 percent of the first molars were Y5 and 22 percent of the second molars were +5 (4 percent were +4, 33 percent were +6). The differences between adults and children are provocative, but the calculated figures are biased by several factors.

TABLE 14 Percentage Distribution of Cusp Patterns on Lower Molars

	Tooth		Number of Cases	Y5	+5	+4	+6	Y6	Irregular
Adults		left	17	100.0	0	0	0	0	0
	M1	right	19	89.5	10.5	0	0	0	0
		total	36	94.4	5.6	0	0	0	0
		left	17	11.8	76.5	11.8	0	0	0
	M2	right	16	12.5	75.0	12.5	0	0	0
		total	33	12.1	75.8	12.1	0	0	0
		left	18	5.6	38.9	11.1	16.7	0	27.8
	M3	right	18	0	38.9	27.8	11.1	0	22.0
		total	36	2.8	38.9	19.4	13.8	0	25.0
Children		left	10	70.0	10.0	0	10.0	10.0	0
	M1	right	7	42.9	14.3	0	28.6	14.3	0
		total	17	58.8	11.8	0	17.6	11.8	0
		left	5	0	20.0	40.0	40.0	0	0
	M2	right	4	0	25.0	50.0	25.0	0	0
		total	9	0	22.2	44.4	33.3	0	0

First, few elderly individuals could be scored, since their teeth were usually too heavily worn to leave any traces of the groove pattern. Furthermore, the groove that separated the hypoconulid and the metaconulid (sixth cusp) on the lower molars of children would tend to be obscured by occlusal attrition by the time they were adults. This may explain why no adult lower first molars were observed to have six cusps, while at least three out of 11 children showed this trait. Perhaps because of this effect, children showed more variability than adults in tooth form of the lower first and second and upper first molars. This may be another example of selection operating to reduce variability in tooth morphology (Perzigian 1975), but because of the uncertain nature of the data, it seems unjustified to do more than make notice of this apparent difference.

The most frequent maxillary cusp patterns were: first molar, 4 (97%); second molar, 3+ (94%); third molar, 3 (46%), 3+ (25%), and 2+ (21%) (Table 15). The first molar pattern differs little from other North American Indian groups (Dahlberg 1951:165). This is not very surprising, since it is the most conservative tooth of the three, according to the principles of the tooth field concept (Dahlberg 1951, 1963). The hypocone is reduced or absent on the second molar more frequently than in the North American Indian groups listed by Dahlberg (1951:166). The difference is probably not statistically significant because of the small sample size for the Powers phase. The third molar is quite variable in form in many populations, and the Powers phase is no exception. It is difficult to compare the data on the Powers phase upper third molars with the information tabulated by Dahlberg (1951:167), since the authors he cited used several different systems for recording tooth form.

As with the mandibular molars, the differences between adults and children for cusp pattern frequencies of the upper second molars are interesting, but the numbers are too small to permit adequate statistical treatment.

DENTAL MEASUREMENTS

In recent years, attention has been drawn to the relationship between advances in food preparation technology and the reduction in size of the human dentition (Brace and Mahler 1971). The summed cross-sectional area of the mandibular and maxillary teeth has been the standard measurement used in studies of post-Pleistocene dental reduction. Because information on tooth areas has not been previously published for the Middle Mississippian period of southeast Missouri, the data for the Powers phase are provided in Tables 16 and 17. The sexes have been pooled in the tables because a large number of the measured dentitions could not be associated with an individual of known sex.

TABLE 15 Percentage Distribution of Cusp Patterns on Upper Molars

	Tooth		N	4	3+	3	2+	Irregular
Adults		left	19	100.0	0	0	0	0
	M1	right	15	93.3	6.7	0	0	0
		total	34	97.0	3.0	0	0	0
		left	18	0	100.0	0	0	0
	M2	right	16	6.2	87.5	6.2	0	0
		total	34	2.9	94.1	2.9	0	0
		left	12	8.3	33.3	41.7	8.3	8.3
	M3	right	12	0	16.7	50.0	33.3	0
		total	24	4.2	25.0	45.8	20.8	4.2
Children		left	9	100.0	0	0	0	0
	M1	right	6	100.0	0	0	0	0
		total	15	100.0	0	0	0	0
		left	5	20.0	20.0	60.0	0	0
	M2	right	6	16.7	33.3	50.0	0	0
		total	11	18.2	27.3	54.5	0	0
	M3	right	1	0	0	100.0	0	0

TABLE 16 Summary Tooth Measurements

	Tooth		Mesio-distal		Bucco-lingual	
		N	X	s	X	s
Mandible	I1	16	5.4	.39	5.8	.27
	I2	25	6.3	.51	6.4	.35
	C	36	7.2	.38	7.8	.48
	P3	35	7.1	.41	8.0	.46
	P4	44	7.1	.42	8.3	.43
	M1	49	11.6	.66	10.9	.45
	M2	52	10.9	.64	10.5	.54
	M3	56	11.2	.92	10.4	.65
Maxilla	I1	13	8.8	.37	7.5	.48
	I2	14	7.5	.50	6.8	.55
	C	25	8.3	.38	8.6	.50
	P3	24	7.3	.34	9.6	.57
	P4	26	6.8	.44	9.2	.47
	M1	44	10.6	.52	11.4	.50
	M2	45	9.9	.62	11.1	.65
	M3	36	9.5	.80	10.6	.76

TABLE 17 Cross-Sectional Areas of the Teeth of the Powers Phase Indians

	Tooth	*Number of Teeth*	*Mean Area*	*Standard Deviation*
Mandible	I1	16	31.3	2.77
	I2	25	40.8	4.42
	C	36	56.2	5.46
	P3	35	57.0	5.47
	P4	44	59.2	5.45
	M1	49	127.2	11.87
	M2	52	114.7	11.60
	M3	56	117.0	15.19
Sum			603.4	
Maxilla	I1	13	66.2	5.10
	I2	14	51.1	7.16
	C	25	71.1	6.04
	P3	24	70.0	6.06
	P4	26	62.6	6.04
	M1	44	121.6	9.72
	M2	45	110.2	11.66
	M3	36	101.4	13.09
Sum			654.2	
Sum (Maxilla and Mandible)			1257.6	

A total of 49 individuals was measured. No individual had a complete dentition, so that the totals for individual teeth are less than the possible maximum of 98 (right and left sides are combined). Average measurement error was determined to be less than 0.1 mm, so measurements were recorded to one decimal place.

DENTAL ANOMALIES

Third molar agenesis was quite rare in this population. In fact, only a single incidence could be found. The third molar was considered to be present in a jaw when the tooth itself, its socket, or its crypt was visible. It was considered absent in adults when the alveolus was present, but showed no traces of antemortem loss of the tooth, and the tooth did not appear in X-rays. Of 27 mandibles where both left and right third molars could be observed, only one–Burial 3 from Snodgrass–lacked a third molar (its right). Eighteen maxillae could be examined for the presence of the third molar on each side, and none lacked it. Eighteen mandibles and ten maxillae could be scored for just one side, and all had the third molar. Thus the third molar was absent in none of the 46 maxillary positions and in just one of 72 (1.4%) mandible halves.

Reduction of size of the third molar may have been occurring, but third molar agenesis seems to be less common than among the populations cited by Dahlberg (1951:171). Only the Blackfoot Indians, among North American populations, are close to the Powers phase figure with eight percent of the dentitions lacking one or more third molars (Dahlberg 1951:171). Caution should be used in the interpretation of these differences since most of the studies cited by Dahlberg did not use X-rays to detect unerupted or impacted teeth which were hidden inside the alveolar bone. One of Dahlberg's sources was Goldstein's (1932) study of Eskimo mandibles. Although Goldstein did not use X-rays himself, he noted that another investigator had used X-rays to study the same jaws and had discovered very few "hidden" third molars. So, it may be that the failure to employ X-rays will not make a major difference in the results.

Most of the cases of anomalies of size and orientation were restricted to the third molars, although there were a few other odd teeth. The upper lateral permanent incisors of Burial 59 from Turner, a 5-year-old child, were peg-shaped. The central incisors were not recovered. Two individuals had supernumerary teeth. Burial 13C, a middle-aged female, had an extra tooth between the right medial and lateral maxillary incisors. The tooth appears similar to a lateral incisor in size, but has less well-developed mesial and distal ridges. It is not a deciduous incisor which failed to exfoliate. Just to the lingual side of the left central incisor is an empty socket, presumably for another supernumerary tooth. This tooth was lost during recovery along with the left central incisor itself. The other supernumerary was an unerupted premolar between the left third and fourth premolars of the mandible designated 61C. The tooth was a fortuitous discovery made when X-rays of the jaw were being taken in order to study the progress of tooth calcification. Other unerupted supernumerary teeth may have been undiscovered because relatively few jaws were X-rayed.

Enamel pearls (Anderson 1969:92; Bass 1971:238) were noted for several individuals. Because enamel pearls are located beneath the neck of the tooth and thus are hidden in the alveolus, they were discovered only when the teeth were free of the bone. For this reason, it would be misleading to compute frequencies of occurrence. A listing of teeth with enamel pearls appears in Table 18. One individual, 13A from Turner, had a small sphere of dentine about 3.5 mm in diameter between the right maxillary fourth premolar and first molar. This was not a pearl connected to either tooth, but may be related to odontomes (dental tumors) as described by Brothwell (1963:154).

TABLE 18 Enamel Pearls

Site	*Burial*	*Individual*	*Tooth*	*Comments*
23BU21B	7	A	RM_2	2 or 3 enamel pearls just off the root tip
23BU21B	7	A	LM^2	
23BU21A	12	A	LM^2	
23BU21A	12	A	RM_2	
23BU21A	17	A	RM_3	
23BU21A	28	?	RM^3	
23BU21A	55	?	RM^2	
23BU21A	55	?	LM^3	

Carabelli's cusp is an accessory cusp found mesially on the lingual surface of the maxillary molars. The cusp itself is usually of low frequency among American Indians, but a related phenomenon, Carabelli's pit, occurs more often. The teeth of Powers phase individuals under age 20 were examined for the trait. Of the eight examined, none had the pit on M^2 or M^3, and two lacked it completely. Of four individuals showing the trait on dm^2, three showed it on M^1. The remaining two individuals lacked the deciduous teeth, but showed the pit on M^1. All these results are consistent with the tooth field concept (Dahlberg 1951:173).

A characteristic considered rare in modern man is the protostylid. It is an extra cusp found on the mesial-buccal surface of the mandibular molar and has its lowest frequency on the first molar. A notable exception to the rarity of this trait is the Pima Indians, 31 percent of whom possess it in varying degrees of prominence on the first molar. Arizona Cliff dwellers, modern Apaches, and modern Pueblo Indians all lack the trait (Dahlberg 1951:162). None of the Powers phase Indians exhibit any development of the protostylid on any of the mandibular molars.

Another characteristic related to the protostylid and manifested in a number of dentitions is a deep buccal pit on the mandibular molars. This could be considered a genetic defect, since it predisposes the affected individual to dental disease, particularly caries (Dahlberg 1951:160). Many cavities of the mandibular molars were seen to have started on the buccal surface; through examination of the dentitions of several individuals, a sequence of development of the buccal caries may be demonstrated. For this reason, this trait was considered together with caries as one type of defective tooth.

DENTAL PATHOLOGY

Individuals who retained their permanent dentitions were divided into three age classes of approximately equal numbers so that some insight into the relationship between age and frequency of dental problems could be gained. The three age classes were 19 to 30, 30 to 41, and 41 to 68 years. Only teeth still in the alveolus were considered, since inclusion of loose teeth would cause problems with misidentification, and because abscesses and antemortem loss can not be investigated on loose teeth. Two different approaches were taken.

In the first approach to dental disease, only individuals with all the molars on one or both sides of a jaw present or accounted for were considered. The number of defective teeth was counted and scored for each individual by age class. For example, B-15, a female from Turner, had all six upper molars and the three right mandibular molars. There were occlusal caries cavities in RM_2, RM_3, and LM^3, and a buccal caries in RM_1. So, her maxilla was scored as one defective tooth in six, while the mandible was three of three. If a tooth was abscessed or lost antemortem, it was also considered to be defective. Size and depth of buccal pits, caries cavities and abscesses were not considered. Defects not visible by macroscopic, surficial examination were not included in either survey, although defects may be identified by other means. For example, abscesses at the root apices which have not "burrowed" through to the surface may be detected by X-rays. This was established with Individual 13C from Turner, who had small abscesses at the tips of both roots of the first right mandibular molar (a tooth with a cavity exposing the pulp chamber). Because of the generally poor preservation of the jaws, it was decided that the expense of X-raying all the jaws outweighted the benefits to be gained by discovering a few invisible abscesses.

The results of the first approach are shown in Tables 19 and 20. In each age class, there were proportionately more mandibles than maxillae with defective teeth. There also appears to be a relationship of progressive dental deterioration with increasing age. One mistake must not be made in evaluating these data: an increase in the number of defective teeth does not equate with

TABLE 19 Number of Defective Teeth in Complete Sets of Molars

	Age Class	*Defective Teeth*						
		0	*1*	*2*	*3*	*4*	*5*	*6*
Mandibular								
	1	2	2	3	0	0	1	0
	2	0	0	2	2	0	1	0
	3	1	2	2	1	1	1	2
Maxillary								
	1	2	0	0	0	0	0	0
	2	2	2	1	1	0	0	0
	3	3	0	0	0	0	0	2

TABLE 20 Number of Defective Teeth in Half Sets of Molars

	Age Class	*Number of Defective Teeth* 0	1	2	3
Mandibular					
	1	3	1	0	0
	2	3	3	0	1
	3	2	2	1	2
Maxillary					
	1	6	1	1	0
	2	3	0	1	0
	3	0	1	0	0

greater pain. An individual (such as B-8B from Turner) with five deep buccal pits, all of which were carious, but none of which reached the pulp cavity, was certainly in less pain than 13C, who had three mandibular caries, two of which reached the pulp cavity. Severity of dental disease does appear to increase with age. This cannot be quantified, however, because it is impossible in some cases to tell whether caries has yet intruded on the pulp cavity. Gross size is no guide, since a very broad cavity may be shallow, while one with a tiny buccal orifice could penetrate very deeply. Clearly, once a caries cavity had started, or an opening for one was provided (as with the buccal pits), the tooth was doomed to rot, become abscessed, and fall out. Only two occurrences interfered with the full development of caries. Heavy tooth wear sometimes wore down an occlusal surface to where a caries cavity was no longer a pocket, but a notch. Ordinary mastication and rinsing of the mouth could then serve to keep it clean, and would slow or stop its development. The most successful means of preventing the full development of caries was an early death. An individual dying in his youth is exposed to less risk of developing caries than a person surviving to age 60.

The second approach to dental disease was not a comparison of partial dentitions by age class, but was instead a lumping together by each tooth of all the individuals in each age class. As before, only teeth still in their sockets were considered. For age classes 1 (19-30 years), 2 (30-41 years), and 3 (41-68) years; 17, 15, and 20 individuals, respectively, were examined. No single kind of tooth was present in all individuals, so that the totals by tooth are smaller than the number of individuals (Table 21). The adult from Burial 4 at Snodgrass, who falls into age class 3, was excluded because he suffered from severe periodontal disease and was just about to lose all of his teeth when he died. Other individuals showing a lesser degree of alveolar resorption were included in the sample.

When the second approach was applied to the mandibular molars, which

TABLE 21 Condition of Individual Teeth by Age Class*

		Left Side					Right Side				
	Tooth	*Good*	*Caries*	*Abscess*	*Caries & Abscess*	*Lost Ante-mortem*	*Good*	*Caries*	*Abscess*	*Caries & Abscess*	*Lost Ante-mortem*
Maxilla	I1	1-3-4	0-0-0	0-0-0	0-0-0	0-0-0	0-3-3	0-0-0	0-0-0	0-0-0	0-0-0
	I2	3-4-4	0-0-1	0-0-0	0-0-0	0-0-0	0-3-2	0-0-0	0-0-0	0-0-0	0-0-0
	C	5-6-6	0-1-0	0-0-0	0-0-0	0-0-0	2-4-4	0-0-0	0-0-0	0-0-0	0-0-0
	P3	8-6-4	0-1-1	0-0-0	0-0-1	0-0-1	2-4-4	0-0-0	0-0-0	0-0-0	0-0-0
	P4	8-6-5	0-1-1	0-0-0	0-0-0	0-0-1	3-5-5	0-0-0	0-0-0	0-0-0	0-0-1
	M1	10-7-4	0-1-0	0-0-0	0-0-0	0-0-1	7-7-5	1-0-0	0-0-0	0-0-0	0-0-1
	M2	11-6-6	0-2-0	0-0-0	0-0-0	0-0-1	7-7-7	1-0-0	0-0-0	0-0-0	0-0-1
	M3	6-4-4	0-4-0	0-0-0	0-0-0	0-0-1	5-6-3	1-1-1	0-0-0	0-0-0	0-0-1
Mandible	I1	3-4-3	0-0-0	0-0-0	0-0-0	0-0-0	3-4-3	0-0-0	0-0-0	0-0-0	0-0-0
	I2	6-4-5	0-0-0	0-0-0	0-0-0	0-0-0	6-5-4	0-0-0	0-0-0	0-0-0	0-0-0
	C	7-7-9	0-0-0	0-0-0	0-0-0	0-0-1	7-7-7	0-0-0	0-0-0	0-0-0	0-0-0
	P3	7-6-7	0-0-2	0-0-1	0-0-0	0-0-0	7-7-6	1-1-1	0-0-1	0-0-0	0-0-1
	P4	9-7-10	0-0-3	0-0-0	0-0-0	0-0-1	7-8-8	1-0-2	0-0-0	1-0-0	0-0-3
	M1	10-5-8	2-3-0	0-0-1	0-0-0	0-0-7	8-7-9	4-3-2	0-0-0	0-0-2	0-1-1
	M2	7-7-8	2-1-0	0-0-0	0-0-1	0-1-8	9-7-7	2-4-0	0-0-0	0-0-1	0-1-4
	M3	9-6-9	3-2-1	0-0-0	0-0-0	0-1-4	8-8-4	3-3-2	0-0-1	0-0-0	0-0-5

*An entry in the table of "4-3-2" means 4, 3 and 2 teeth, respectively, from the jaws of individuals in age classes 1, 2 and 3. Age class 1 is the youngest group, aged 19 to 30 years. Individuals in age class 2 are aged between 30 and 41 years. Age class 3 is the oldest class, aged 41 to 68 years. The age classes include approximately equal numbers of individuals.

are best represented and most often diseased, further evidence for the contention that teeth are worst in the oldest individuals was found. The percentage of carious and abscessed teeth declines from about 26 percent in the first two age classes to 13 percent in the third, but the frequency of teeth lost before death climbs from 0 percent in the first to 7 percent in the second to 34 percent in the third age class. A similar relationship between caries and antemortem tooth loss was recorded by Goldstein (1948:69) for a series of crania from Texas. In that sample, caries frequency increased until age 35 and then decreased. However, the increase in antemortem tooth loss more than made up for the decrease in caries, so that there was an overall increase in dental disease.

In order to get caries information comparable to published charts (Brothwell 1963; Phenice 1969b), the same individuals were re-examined using the second approach, this time with loose teeth included. Teeth with abscesses but no caries were considered healthy. Even with loose teeth included, the single-rooted teeth were under-represented. Thus, the overall figure of 11.6 percent caries is misleading because the more frequently carious molars outnumber of all other kinds of teeth. If the frequency of caries is recalculated by averaging the percentages of caries at each of the 16 tooth positions, the result is the slightly lower figure of 9.9 percent caries. This is much higher than the similarly calculated values of 2.9 percent for the Sully site, a protohistoric site in Kansas, and 6.4 percent for the Woodland Schultz mounds of northeastern Kansas (Phenice 1969b). However, the caries percentages for these two North American Plains populations are probably depressed by their high rates of antemortem tooth loss. The Powers phase caries rate is closer to those for Greece (12.1%) and Crete (9.0%) in the period 3000-1000 B.C. Brothwell (1963:275) gives 3.1 percent caries as an average value for seven European, one Egyptian, and one Chinese samples from the period 3000-1000 B.C. The Powers phase figure greatly exceeds this, but much of the difference may be dependent on individual differences in assessing the condition of the teeth. Brothwell (1963:273) says that only well-defined cavities are ordinarily recorded. As previously noted, many of the cavities in the Powers phase teeth were quite small. Because of this, the calculated frequency of caries may be less of an underestimate than is usually the case.

Brothwell (1963:276) also reported the percentage of caries, tooth by tooth, for three populations (Table 22). He notes that the second molar consistently has a higher frequency of caries than the first molar. A chi-square test of his data, however, shows that this frequency difference is significant at the $p \leqslant .05$ level for only the Middle Minoan sample. Furthermore, no allowance is made for the teeth lost before death because of abscesses. This factor becomes increasingly important as the average age of the population

TABLE 22 Incidence of Dental Caries in Four Populations with Reference to Differences Among Teeth*

	Middle Minoans			*French Neolithic*			*26th-30th Dynasty Egyptians*			*Powers Phase Indians*		
Tooth	*N*	*% Caries*	*Rank*	*N*	*% Caries*	*Rank*	*N*	*% Caries*	*Rank*	*N*	*% Caries*	*Rank*
I1	112	1.8	1	992	0.3	1	120	0.0	1	50	0.0	1
I2	113	8.0	5	1067	1.0	3	130	0.0	2	63	3.2	3
C	203	5.4	2	1395	0.4	2	153	0.7	4	88	1.1	2
P3	189	8.5	6	1630	1.8	4	226	1.8	5	94	9.6	4
P4	194	6.7	3	1479	3.2	5	229	0.4	3	103	11.7	5
M1	268	7.5	4	1961	5.5	7	327	3.4	7	112	17.0	7
M2	280	12.9	7	1914	6.0	8	339	5.3	8	110	13.6	6
M3	146	18.5	8	279	4.7	6	218	2.3	6	104	24.0	8
Combined anterior	428	5.1		3454	0.6		303	0.0		201	1.5	
Combined premolar	383	7.6		3109	2.4		455	1.1		197	10.7	
Combined molar	694	12.0		4154	5.7		884	3.8		326	18.1	

*After Brothwell (1963:276)

increases. If the Powers phase material is any indication, the oldest third of the adult population will appear to have fewer cavities than the younger two-thirds if tooth loss is not considered. When the Powers phase Indians are compared to the three populations of Brothwell's Table II (Table 22), the rank order of caries frequency by tooth is very similar, especially to the French Neolithic sample, although the absolute frequencies match best with the Middle Minoan sample. If the teeth are combined into three still more inclusive groups, the anterior teeth, the premolars, and the molars, all four populations conform to ordinary expectations. The teeth with the most complicated crowns, the molars, are most often carious, followed by the premolars and the anterior teeth, in that order.

The general abundance of caries in the teeth of the Powers phase Indians suggests that they had a fair amount of sugar in their diet. The proportional composition of their diet is unknown. However, large quantities of burned seeds and nut shells attest to the use of maize, (*Zea mays*), hickory nuts, (*Carya* sp.), marsh elder (*Iva annua* var. *macrocarpa*), acorns (*Quercus* sp.), common beans (*Phaseolus vulgaris*), and pecans (*Carya illinoensis*). Other plants represented in smaller quantities are walnuts (*Juglans nigra*), wild beans (*Strophostyles* sp.), persimmons (*Diospyros virginiana*), and squash (*Cucurbita* sp.). Paul Minnis (personal communication) determined the weight of the burned seeds and shells from four pits on the Turner site. Maize kernels outweighed all other types of plant remains by about nine to one (11.2 kg to 1.2 kg). When maize is cooked, its starch is converted to sugar. If cooked maize were an important part of the diet, then it would have been a major source of sugar.

The advent of maize agriculture in this region may have led to an increased consumption of sugar, and hence, to an increased frequency of caries. To test this proposition, a comparison of the Powers phase Indians with non-agricultural groups of the same genetic stock should be made. The genetic relationship is necessary to help control for factors such as the presence of antibodies to oral bacteria in the saliva. No large pre-agricultural skeletal populations are yet available for the Powers phase areas, but some may become available with continued excavations in the region.

A better understanding of prehistoric dietary regimes may become possible with the development of techniques such as the analysis of the strontium and carbon isotope contents of human bone. Strontium analysis is used to gain insight into the proportion of meat in the diet (Brown 1973). The importance of maize in the diet may be estimated from the ratio of ^{13}C to ^{12}C in bone collagen (Vogel and Van der Merwe 1976). When used in conjunction with each other, these two techniques may provide much information on the composition of the diet of a prehistoric people.

The teeth were examined for indications of periodontal disease, calculus deposits (tartar), and lines of enamel hypoplasia. Periodontal disease is an infection of the soft tissues of the mouth and of the alveolar bone. It causes the bone to recede by degrees, loosening the teeth, and finally causing their loss. Brothwell (1965:149) lists unclean mouths, irritation by calculus deposits, attrition, and lowered tissue resistance through a faulty diet as contributing factors. Of 43 adults examined, ten showed some degree of alveolar resorption, and nine of these also had calculus deposits on the teeth. Fourteen other individuals showed traces of tartar, but no alveolar resorption, while the remaining 19 showed neither. Tartar may have been scraped off some teeth during cleaning in the lab, reducing the number of individuals apparently affected. A continuity-corrected chi-square test of a fourfold table for association of calculus with alveolar resorption yielded a test value of 5.20, which is significant at $p \leqslant .025$ (Table 23).

TABLE 23 Test of Association of Alveolar Resorption with Dental Calculus

		Resorption		
		Present	*Absent*	*Total*
Calculus	Present	9	14	23
	Absent	1	19	20
	Total	10	33	43

The frequency of calculus occurrence appears to increase with age, as does periodontal disease. When the data are divided into three age classes, the association between age, calculus, and alveolar resorption becomes clear (Table 24). A chi-square test of the relationship between age and alveolar resorption showed that association between them could not be rejected (Table 25). However, a similar test rejected the association between calculus and age at the $p = .05$ level (Table 26). It may be said that roughly half the adult population had tartar on its teeth, and about half of this number had some degree of periodontal disease. However, in view of the association between age and alveolar resorption, this figure should be used with caution in any comparisons to other populations.

Macroscopic enamel hypoplasia refers to pits or transverse grooves occurring on the teeth. These minor defects are thought to result from various systemic disturbances occurring during childhood when the tooth crowns are calcifying (Kreshover 1960), and so may be related to the lines and bands of increased density (Harris lines) occurring in the long bones. Much work relating Harris lines to the incidence of disease has been done with living and skeletal populations (Allison, Mendoza and Pezzia 1974; Blanco, Acheson, Canosa, and Salomon 1974; Dreizen, Currie, Gilley, and Spies 1956; Marshall 1968; McHenry 1968). Unfortunately, no radiopaque lines could be observed on the X-rays of the best preserved long bones from the Powers phase sites, so no comparison of the timing of enamel hypoplasia and Harris lines could be made.

TABLE 24 Association of Alveolar Resorption and Dental Calculus by Age Class

Age Class	*No Resorption or Calculus*	*Calculus But No Resorption*	*Resorption But No Calculus*	*Calculus And Resorption*
1	9	4	0	0
2	5	8	0	0
3	5	2	1	9

TABLE 25 Test of Association of Alveolar Resorption with Age

		Resorption		
		Present	*Absent*	*Total*
Age Class	1 and 2	0	26	26
	3	10	7	17
	Total	10	33	43

TABLE 26 Test of Association of Calculus with Age

		Calculus		
		Present	*Absent*	*Total*
Age Class	1	4	9	13
	2	8	5	13
	3	12	5	17
	Total	24	19	43

Working with children from Heliconia, Colombia, Stini (1969) showed that the combination of poor diet after weaning, parasites, diarrhea, and infections produced severe physiological stress which interfered with growth and sometimes resulted in death. If the Powers phase people tended to wean their infants at the same age and gave them an inferior diet, then the teeth may show hypoplastic lines which could be used together with calcification standards (Moorrees, Fanning, and Hunt 1963) to infer the age at which weaning was practiced. Since most individuals have multiple sets of hypoplastic lines, it is difficult to associate any particular line with a particular cause. If, however, a large number of individuals show the same lines of hypoplasia, then this might be construed as evidence of a common cause. The argument is not strong, and the problem would be better tested with a modern sample where records of weaning age have been kept.

Since the published calcification standards (Moorrees, Fanning, and Hunt 1963) for tooth crowns are complete for only the lower teeth, exclusive of the incisors, only these teeth were examined. In no case were lines observed in the upper half of a tooth crown, even when other teeth showed lines at an equivalent age on the lower halves of their crowns. Some individuals had only a few teeth sufficiently clean and well-preserved to permit identification of lines, but every individual showed lines on at least one tooth. In older individuals, occlusal wear removes much of the crown, thereby destroying lines relating to earlier episodes. The situation was further complicated because when lines were recognized, they often appeared as broad bands, and so could not be assigned to a particular age. The result is that the most sensitive indicator is to compare the frequencies at which different teeth were affected, not the estimated age for each line (Table 27). If the frequencies of hypoplastic teeth are ordered by the midpoint of the age range between half and complete calcification of the crown (since no lines were found in the upper half of the tooth crowns), the curve clearly peaks with the canines at age 2.8, then declines (Fig. 6).

The first molar (midpoint 1.4 years) calcifies before the canine, and the third premolar (midpoint 4.2 years) calcifies next after the canine. If this peak has anything to do with weaning, it suggests that the age of weaning is

TABLE 27 Frequencies of Hypoplastic Teeth

Tooth	*Number Examined*	*Number of Hypoplastic Teeth*	*Proportion of Hypoplastic Teeth*
C	36	34	.94
P_3	32	13	.41
P_4	29	9	.31
M_1	35	15	.43
M_2	24	8	.33
M_3	19	5	.26

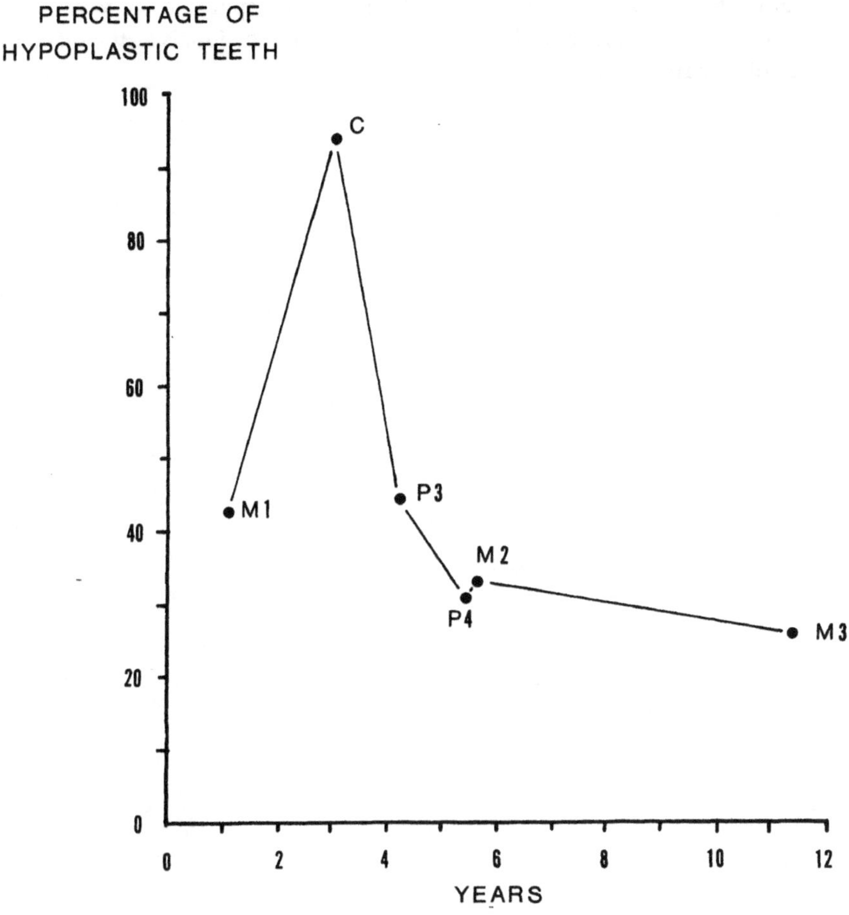

FIGURE 7
INCIDENCE OF ENAMEL HYPOPLASIA BY AGE

Figure 6. Incidence of Enamel Hypoplasia by Age

between one and a half and four years. On the other hand, the sole significance may be that hypoplastic lines are most easily detected on the canine. It is important to note here that the calcification standards were derived from a modern White population and may not be strictly applicable; however, they do serve to give a general indication of the ages of individuals at the different stages of calcification.

4

The Social Analyses

Demography

A life table (Table 28) for the individuals of known age from the Turner site was constructed following the techniques outlined by Weiss (1973). Only individuals aged by the dentition were included in the table. It is assumed that the population structure was relatively stable during the deposition of the cemetery.

A correction in the raw mortality data was made before the life table was constructed. Following Asch (1973), each individual was uniformly distributed over several age classes according to the error assigned to his age. An individual aged 48 ±10 years would be divided up as 0.1 in the 35 to 40 class, 0.25 in each of the 40 to 45, 45 to 50, and 50 to 55 classes, and 0.15 in the 55 to 60 age class. This smoothes the mortality curve and helps to remove the aura of false precision created by strictly assigning the 48-year-old to the 45 to 50 class.

No children aged less than one year were recovered from the cemetery. Their absence causes a very unusual life table. Two important statistics are unaffected by the missing infants: ${}_nq_x$, the probability of dying between ages x and $x+n$, and $e^\circ(x)$, the life expectancy at age x. All other statistics are over-estimates, since they assume 100 percent survivorship to age one year, because no correction has been made for the missing infants in Table 28.

An estimate of the number of infant deaths was necessary to correct these other statistics and to put the life table in a form which could be compared to Weiss's (1973) model tables.

Several prehistoric life tables which had been constructed for North American Indians were examined in order to find an appropriate value for ${}_1q_0$ or for the number of deaths in the age interval from birth to one year. Blakely's (1971) mortality rates for a Middle Mississippian population from Dickson Mounds, Illinois, were surprisingly close to those for Turner. His

TABLE 28 Uncorrected Life Table for the Turner Cemetery

Age	*D(x)*	*d(x)*	*l(x)*	*Q(x)*	*L(x)*	*T(x)*	$\overset{\circ}{e}(x)$
0							
1	5.083	7.94	100.00	.0794	384.120	2707.270	27.07
5	8.784	13.72	92.06	.1490	426.000	2323.150	25.24
10	2.558	4.00	78.34	.0510	381.700	1897.150	24.22
15	4.949	7.73	74.34	.1040	352.375	1515.450	20.38
20	7.325	11.45	66.61	.1719	304.425	1163.075	17.46
25	6.207	9.70	55.16	.1758	251.550	858.650	15.57
30	7.263	11.35	45.46	.2496	198.925	607.100	13.35
35	5.875	9.18	34.11	.2691	147.600	408.175	11.97
40	5.244	8.19	24.93	.3285	104.175	260.575	10.45
45	3.780	5.91	16.74	.3530	68.925	156.400	9.34
50	2.537	3.96	10.83	.3656	44.250	87.475	8.08
55	2.200	3.44	6.87	.5007	25.750	43.225	6.29
60	1.350	2.11	3.43	.6152	11.875	17.475	5.09
65	.550	.86	1.32	.6515	4.450	5.600	4.24
70	.250	.40	.46	1.0000	1.150	1.150	2.50
75	0	0	0	0	0	0	0

table was divided into ten-year age classes, so the Turner data were put into this form for purposes of comparison (Table 29). A chi-square test was used to compare the age distributions of deaths of the two populations, excluding the 0 to 9 class. The hypothesis that the two distributions were the same could not be rejected at the $p=.05$ level. The age distributions of deaths were then compared in a four-fold table, using the age classes 0-9 and 10+ (Table 30). This time, the hypothesis of identical age distributions was rejected at the .05 level.

The differences in the mortality patterns between Dickson Mounds and Turner were assumed to be due solely to the lack of infants in the Turner sample for three reasons. First, the mortality rates for the Turner age classes 1-4, 5-9, and 10-14 conformed fairly well with the shape of model life tables (Weiss 1973; Coale and Demeny 1966). Second, the adult mortality patterns had already been shown to be quite similar. Third, no infants had been included in the Turner sample. Since 64.7 percent of the Dickson Mounds deaths occurred after age ten, it was presumed that the 50.1 deaths that occurred after age ten in the Turner sample also represented 64.7 percent of the deaths there. The total number of deaths which should have been represented at Turner was then calculated to be 50.1 ÷ .647 = 77.4. This was

TABLE 29 Comparison of Turner and Dickson Mounds Mortality: Ages 10 and Over

Site	*Age Class*						
	10-19	*20-29*	*30-39*	*40-49*	*50-59*	*60-79*	*Total*
Turner	7.5	13.5	13.1	9.0	4.7	2.2	50.0
Dickson Mounds	46.0	74.0	76.0	70.0	25.0	19.0	310.0
Total	53.5	87.5	89.1	79.0	29.7	21.2	360.0
	x^2=.929		df=5		Not Significant		

TABLE 30 Comparison of Turner and Dickson Mounds Mortality: All Ages

Site	*Age Class*		
	0-9	*10+*	*Total*
Turner	13.867	50.088	63.955
Dickson Mounds	169.0	310.0	479.0
Total	182.867	360.088	542.955
x^2=4.671	df=1	$.025<p<.05$	

rounded up to 78. The 63.955 deaths included in the Turner life table were subtracted from 78 to yield 14.045 infant deaths (Table 28).

A new life table was then constructed to include the estimated infant deaths (Table 31). This was then compared to a number of Weiss's model tables which appeared similar in form. The statistic compared was $C(x)$, the percentage distribution of ages of the living populations represented by the life tables. This statistic is calculated for a stationary, stable population by dividing $L(x)$, the man-years lived in age class x, by $e^{\circ}(O)$, the life expectancy at birth. The Turner age distribution was compared to the model tables using two different methods: a chi-square test and the "Index of Dissimilarity."

With the chi-square test, almost all the model tables were accepted as not significantly different from the observed age distribution, but the lowest values of chi-square were found for the *MT:20-X* series, in which life expectancy at 15 years of age is 20 years, and *X* is the proportion surviving to age 15. All of these model tables had chi-square values between 1.76 and 2.09 (with 10 degrees of freedom).

Weiss advocates the Index of Dissimilarity as the measure for selecting the best-fitting model table. The index is merely the sum of the absolute values of the differences between the observed and model values of C(x). Weiss notes that an index value "smaller than .1 is a good fit by general standards and surely by anthropological standards" (1973:65). This is quite an understatement, since the model values of $C(x)$ are printed to just one decimal place accuracy, so any value smaller than 0.1 would have to be a perfect fit. Perhaps he meant 1.0, which is still a very close fit, particularly for ungraduated field data. The lowest index values for the Turner data were with the *MT:20-X* series. The three best-fitting model tables and their values for the Index of Dissimilarity were: *MT:20-60*, *8.1*; *MT:20-55*, *8.5*; and *MT:20-65*, *8.6*. Of these, *MT:20-60* fits best for 11 other statistics derived from the life table (Table 32).

The main element contributing to the high values for the index is the rather heavy adult mortality of the Turner life table. This, in turn, is the result of a deficit of elderly individuals among the burials at Turner. The early French adventurers reported encounters with very old Indians in the region south of Missouri (DuPratz in Swanton 1911:108). Although their accounts did not describe the Powers phase Indians in particular, the existence of aged Indians elsewhere increases the probability that there were aged Indians in Missouri. The reason for the lack of elderly individuals among the burials is hard to explain, unless it is caused by an error in sampling. There are four possible sources for this error.

The first source of error is related to the pioneering nature of the Powers phase Mississippian occupation. It is possible that the initial group that moved

TABLE 31 Corrected Life Table for the Turner Cemetery

Age	*D(x)*	*d(x)*	*l(x)*	*Q(x)*	*L(x)*	*T(x)*	$\mathring{e}(x)$
0	14.045	18.006	100.000	.1801	88.2961	2301.2312	23.01
1	5.083	6.517	81.994	.0795	310.7776	2212.9351	26.99
5	8.784	11.262	75.477	.1492	349.2300	1902.1575	25.20
10	2.558	3.279	64.215	.0511	312.8775	1552.9275	24.18
15	4.949	6.345	60.936	.1041	288.8175	1240.0500	20.35
20	7.325	9.391	54.591	.1720	249.4775	951.2325	17.42
25	6.207	7.958	45.200	.1761	206.1050	701.7550	15.52
30	7.263	9.312	37.242	.2500	162.9300	495.6500	13.31
35	5.875	7.532	27.930	.2697	120.8200	332.7200	11.91
40	5.244	6.723	20.398	.3296	85.1825	211.9000	10.39
45	3.780	4.846	13.675	.3544	56.2600	126.7175	9.27
50	2.537	3.253	8.829	.3684	36.0125	70.4575	7.98
55	2.200	2.820	5.576	.5057	20.8300	34.4450	6.18
60	1.350	1.731	2.756	.6281	9.4525	13.6150	4.94
65	.550	.705	1.025	.6878	3.3625	4.1625	4.06
70	.250	.320	.320	1.0000	.8000	.8000	2.50
75	0	0	0	0	0	0	0

TABLE 32 Model Life Table MT: 20.0-60.0*

Age	*Q(x)*	*1(x)*	*L(x)*	*T(x)*	$E^{\circ}(x)$	*C(x)*
0	.2000	100.0	87	2226	22.3	3.9
1	.1200	80.0	295	2139	26.7	13.2
5	.0910	70.4	336	1844	26.2	15.1
10	.0624	64.0	310	1508	23.6	13.9
15	.1905	60.0	271	1198	20.0	12.2
20	.1970	48.6	218	927	19.1	9.8
25	.2038	39.0	175	709	18.2	7.8
30	.2108	31.1	138	535	17.2	6.2
35	.2180	24.5	109	396	16.2	4.9
40	.2254	19.2	85	287	15.0	3.8
45	.2330	14.8	65	203	13.7	2.9
50	.2409	11.4	50	138	12.1	2.2
55	.2812	8.6	37	88	10.2	1.7
60	.3646	6.2	25	51	8.1	1.1
65	.4546	3.9	15	25	6.4	0.7
70	.5738	2.2	8	10	4.6	0.3
75	1.0000	0.9	2	2	2.5	0.1
80	0.0	0.0	0	0	0.0	0.0

Crude Birth Rate	.0449	Proportion Under 15	46.2
Index of Growth Regulation	1.0143	Proportion 15 to 50	47.6
Completed Family Size	2.92	Proportion Over 50	6.2
Mean Family Size	3.33	Dependency Ratio	1.1
Generation Length	26.69	Average Age	20.3
Adult Survivorship	19.0	Average of Adults	31.6

*After Weiss (1973:130)

in may have left the old and infirm behind with other kinsmen. If this were the case, the population would not have been stable in the demographic sense, because the age distribution would have slowly changed until the elderly once again regained their former proportions in the population. There would have been an initial deficit of deaths of the very aged causing an increase in the apparent mortality of younger adults and a decrease in the apparent longevity of the Turner occupants. Unfortunately, without age and sex information for the complete population, it is impossible to do more than state this as an untestable possibility.

The second possible cause is related to the first one. Perhaps the achievements of a lifetime entitled some of the elderly to be buried at another location. The effect of this practice would be to increase the apparent mortality at the donor site and to decrease it at the recipient site. Three of the five adults recovered from burials at Powers Fort were old males. This unex-

pectedly high proportion of elderly individuals is provocative, but, because
adults recovered from burials at Powers Fort were old males. This unexpectedly high proportion of elderly individuals is provocative, but, because the sample is so small, it is unreasonable to attribute any significance to it. A similar effect could be caused by the death and disposal of adults while they were away from Turner. Any activity which took people far enough from the site to make it inconvenient to carry back a corpse could contribute to this situation.

A third cause could be simple stochastic variation of mortality rates around the stable values. This variation was shown to be a significant factor in small populations such as Turner (Moore, Swedlund, and Armelagos 1975). The effect may have caused the unusual mortality figures observed by Ubelaker in the late prehistoric ossuaries he reported from Maryland (1974:62-63). Perhaps the complete excavation of several other Powers phase cemeteries could shed light on the problem of stochastic variation.

The fourth possible cause for the lack of elderly individuals may be dealt with more easily. Since the individual ages were based on attrition of the molars, individuals lacking the molars were of necessity omitted. A number of these were individuals who had lost most of their teeth to periodontal disease or abscesses. The number of defective teeth has been shown to increase with age, as has the incidence of periodontal disease. Thus, there is every reason to expect those individuals who have lost their molars to periodontal disease and abscesses to be among the most aged in the population. Of the 45 individuals from Turner who were aged by dental wear, only one was over 60. It is quite possible that the apparent high mortality of the adults at Turner is an artifact of the aging method used and does not represent the real mortality of these age classes.

Given the number of assumptions already involved in constructing the Turner life table, there is little loss of accuracy in adopting Weiss's model table *MT:20-60*. His model tables have the advantage of being calculated from a sample composed of many sizable populations, both prehistoric and historic from around the world, thus avoiding the problem created by the small, sexually biased Turner sample. The Turner sample population has proved sufficient to allow the connection with a better life table to be made.

Of the extra statistics provided with Weiss's model life tables, most are self-explanatory. The "Index of Growth Regulation" is a measure of the relative importance of mortality among reproducing females versus the importance of reduction of fertility to levels less than the human maximum. Values less than one show mortality to be the dominant mechanism of growth regulation, while values greater than one show the increasing importance of fertility reduction. The statistic is primarily of recent historical interest, and has no importance in this study. "Completed Family Size (Gross Reproductive Rate)" refers to the number of female births to a woman surviving to age 50. "Mean Family Size" is the number of children of both sexes born to the average woman. It is less than twice the GRR, since few women survive from 15 to 50 (19 percent in this model population). The "Dependency Ratio" is the ratio of the number of individuals under 15 or over 50 to the number between those ages. In the case of *MT:20-60*, every person between the age of 15 and 50 is responsible for an average of 1.1 dependents. Weiss draws a sharp distinction between average age and life expectancy at birth. It is true that in most of his tables these values are different. However, in a stationary population, the two should be identical. The differences are probably due to various functions used to smooth the life table and to rounding errors.

The model life table may now be used in an attempt to determine whether the cemetery at Turner contains only the deceased occupants of the site, or whether other groups also buried their dead at Turner. In a stationary population, the total number of man-years lived by a population over a specified period of time should equal the total number of man-years lived during the lives of those dying during the same period (Asch 1973:116). If it is assumed that all of the Turner site dead were buried within the confines of the village, an estimate of the total number of man-years lived by the contemporary village can be made.

Fragments of 118 individuals aged 1.75 to 65 have been recovered from the Turner cemetery (113 were identified from bones in the lab; one adult, one juvenile, and three individuals of unknown age were identified in the field but were not saved (Appendix C). Although only one infant burial was found beneath a house floor at Turner, evidence from other Powers phase sites suggests this was the standard place of interment for those aged less than one year. Since infants do not contribute significantly to the man-years statistic, and since their absence has been compensated in the life table, infant underrepresentation is no problem.

Missing adults are a real problem, since the man-years figure is largely dependent on the adult deaths. The adoption of the model life table should correct for this difficulty, if the lack of old adults is due only to the use of dental attrition as the aging technique. If a substantial number of adults from Turner were buried elsewhere or were disposed of by a means other than interment, then their absence will not have been compensated by the model life table. Were that the case, a less conservative life table would have been appropriate for the population. If the apparent imbalance in the sex ratio is not due to sexing errors or random causes (the probability of a sample of 87 people drawn from a population containing 50 percent men and 50 percent women having 65.5 percent or more females is .002), and if male infanticide were not being practiced, then there is a possibility that male corpses were disposed of elsewhere. Perhaps war casualties could not always be recovered, or males who died on hunting forays were buried on the spot. The effect of each of these events would be to reduce the total number of man-years represented in the Turner cemetery. The only way to increase the man-years figure is to bury outsiders in the Turner cemetery. Thus, an excess of man-years represented by burials at Turner over other estimates of man-years at the site may be explained only as the result of the burial of outsiders in the cemetery, whereas a deficit may occur in many different ways.

Only 64 of the minimum of 118 individuals in the Turner cemetery could be aged by tooth calcification or attrition. For the other 54, only the proportions of adults and juveniles are known. Most of the 54 were adults, because adult skeletons preserve better than those of children. Some adults were identified from just a few post-cranial bones to which no age could be applied. By contrast, several child burials were represented by teeth only. However, since the presence of a few of a child's teeth is sufficient to allow the child to be identified and aged, most of the children that were identified were also aged. Children do not contribute significantly to the man-years figure, so over-estimating or under-estimating their number is not a real concern here. It is much more important to get an accurate estimate of the adult population. For this reason, the total man-years represented by the Turner cemetery is derived by two methods.

The first method is based only on the total number of individuals recognized, 118, and ignores the problem just raised above. A chi-square test comparing the adult and juvenile distributions of the demographic sample (49 adults, 15 children) and the remainder of the population (43 adults, 8 children, 3 unknown age) showed no significant difference at the $p=.05$ level. This justified ignoring the difference in the age distributions of the two samples. Since the total man-years in the model life table (2226) is based on a population of 100, a population of 118 would have lived 1.18 times as many years, or 2627 man-years.

Alternatively, a higher estimate of total man-years could be made by multiplying the number of child burials times the average age of the dead children (aged 1 to 15–infants make virtually no contribution to man-years and were not among the 23 children) and by multiplying the number of adult burials times the average age of adults, and then summing the two figures. For the purpose of this estimate, the three individuals of unknown age from B-1 and B-13 are assumed to be adults. The average age of children aged 1 to 15 may be calculated from the life table as

$$\sum_{1}^{15} \bar{x}\, C(x) \,/\, C(1,15) = 7.74$$

years. The number of man-years lived by children is equal to *23x7.74*, or 178. Two different adult figures may be calculated, one based on average age of adults and one on life expectancy at 15. These should be equal, as noted earlier for age and life expectancy at birth. The average age of adults is given in the model table as 31.6, whereas 15-year-olds may expect to survive to 35. These two figures, multiplied by 95 adults, give 3002 and 3325 man-years, respectively. The combined adult and juvenile figures are then 3180 and 3503 man-years, respectively. Ignoring the problem of burials which may have been plowed completely away, since there were probably very few of them, 3500 man-years can be considered to be a maximum for the Turner site cemetery, and 2630 man-years to be a minimum.

Now, an estimate of the total man-years lived by the Turner population while they inhabited the site is needed. The estimate is actually the product of two other estimates: average population of the site, and average length of occupation of a structure. Three methods of estimating population for the Turner site are presented below together with an estimate of the length of the Turner occupation.

The first method of determining population is Naroll's floor area approach (1962). House floor areas were available for 39 of the 43 structures at Turner. The total area under these structure roofs was 1175 m^2. This may be substituted into Naroll's equation as follows:

$$\text{Population} = \text{antilog}\,\frac{(\log F - 1.33646)}{0.84195} = \text{antilog}\,\frac{(\log 1175 - 1.33646)}{0.84195} = 115$$

This figure appears to underestimate the probable average population at Turner, since it would allow for less than three people per measured structure. Multiplying the population by the years of occupancy of the site gives an estimate of the total man-years lived at Turner.

Another method of estimating population was developed by Cook and Heizer (1968) following their investigations of California sites. They allowed 20 $ft.^2$ of floor space per occupant for each of the first six people in a structure, and 100 $ft.^2$ for each additional occupant. This procedure yields an estimate of 310 for the maximum Turner population, an average of over seven inhabitants per structure. This may be compared with Cook and Heizer's statement (1968:89) that a family size of six was almost universal in California, as well as with Swanton's figures showing an estimate of slightly over eight people per cabin for a number of tribes in the Southeast (1911:43). However, the cabins to which Swanton referred tended to be a bit larger than those at the Turner site. The cabins of the Natchez ranged from 15 ft.

on a side to over 30 ft. on a side (Swanton 1911:43). The mean structure area at Turner was 324 ft.^{2}, and ranged from a low of 136 to a high of 676 ft.^{2} (Black 1972). Thus, an estimate of fewer than eight people per structure for Turner would be appropriate, if the number of occupants were related to structure size.

By assuming that each structure at Turner was occupied by a nuclear family and by multiplying the average family size by the number of structures, another estimate of the population of the site may be made. Multiplying this figure by the average number of years of occupancy of a structure produces an estimate of the total number of man-years lived on the Turner site. This is called the "structure-number" approach (Black 1973). A good estimate of the nuclear family size can be derived from the Mean Family Size of the model life table. This figure, 3.33, is the mean number of male and female children which must be born to each woman reaching age 15 in order for the population to remain stable and stationary. If both parents are assumed to be alive and residing with the children under a single roof, then the "mean family" would be 5.33. A mean family size of five will be assumed to be the best estimate, although the contingency table constructed to estimate man-years from the structure-number approach will allow the number of inhabitants per structure to range from three to eight.

The remaining step is to estimate the average duration of occupancy for a structure on the Turner site. At first, it would seem that what is wanted is an estimate of the length of occupation of the site, but this is not so. Consider the admittedly absurd situation where the structures were occupied sequentially, one at a time. If each of the approximately 40 domiciliary structures at Turner were occupied for 2.5 years, then the whole site would have been inhabited for 100 years. This span of time exceeds the estimate for the duration of the entire Powers phase (Price 1973). Multiplying 100 years times the population estimate derived from the Cook and Heizer (1968) method would yield a figure of 31,000 man-years at the site. This requires 310 people to occupy each structure and is clearly nonsensical. However, if the average occupancy span for a structure is multiplied by the maximum population estimate, a much more reasonable estimate of total man-years on the site can be obtained. This is not a trivial point, since it has been suggested that certain parts of the Turner site were abandoned before others. Thus, even if the maximum population of 310 computed by the Cook and Heizer method is correct, it is quite possible that the largest contemporary population was only 100 individuals. Using the average time of occupancy of a structure obviates the problem of contemporaneity.

Only one structure at Turner was in use long enough to require the rebuilding of its walls, while several other structures were either unoccupied or were abandoned soon after occupation. James B. Griffin and James E. Price both believe that the houses at Turner might have survived two or three years without needing rebuilding, but probably not as many as five years (Griffin: personal communication; Price: personal communication). Furthermore, the accumulation of debris on the site is not great enough to indicate more than a brief occupation.

Contingency tables for estimating the total man-years lived by the Turner inhabitants are presented for each of the three approaches (Tables 33 and 34).

The hypothesis that the Turner cemetery served more than just the inhabitants of the Turner site for the period of time they lived there may now be tested. The null hypothesis is that the Turner dead represent only the occupants of the site who died while it was inhabited. The alternative hypothesis is that the cemetery was in use by more people than lived at Turner or for a longer period of time than Turner was occupied, or both. If the estimates of man-years computed for the site exceed or equal those computed for the cemetery, the null hypothesis will be accepted. If the contrary is true, the null hypothesis will be rejected in favor of the alternative.

The minimum and maximum estimates of man-years based on the cemetery data were 2630 and 3500. The estimates of man-years derived from the Naroll approach are all much smaller than the cemetery estimates (Table 33).

TABLE 33 Man-Years at Turner Derived from Two Population Estimates

Method of Estimating Population	Years of Occupancy				
	1	*2.5*	*5.0*	*7.5*	*10*
Naroll (1962)	115	288	575	862	1150
Cook and Heizer (1968)	310	775	1550	2325	3100

TABLE 34 Man-Years at Turner Derived from the Structure/Number Approach

Years of Occupancy	Occupants Per Structure					
	3	*4*	*5*	*6*	*7*	*8*
2.5	300	400	500	600	700	800
5.0	600	800	1000	1200	1400	1600
7.5	900	1200	1500	1800	2100	2400
10.0	1200	1600	2000	2400	2800	3200

All the estimates based on the Cook and Heizer approach are smaller, except the ten year occupancy estimate, which exceeds the minimum cemetery estimate (Table 33). In the structure-number approach table, only two figures (for ten years, and seven or eight occupants) exceed the minimum cemetery estimate, and none exceeds the maximum (Table 34). However, since the ten year occupancy estimate has already been rejected as extremely unlikely, the null hypothesis is rejected.

The Snodgrass site is quite close to Turner (about 200 yds.) but has no cemetery. It may prove informative to calculate a few man-year estimates based on the assumption that both Snodgrass and Turner used the Turner cemetery. Snodgrass has about 90 domiciliary structures. With the Cook and Heizer method, the population at Snodgrass may be estimated at 626. Naroll's method will not be used again because it seriously underestimated the population at Turner. Since there is no more evidence of a long occupation at Snodgrass than there is at Turner, the same estimates of the period of use of a structure will be employed.

Examination of Tables 35 and 36 shows that Turner and Snodgrass combined could account for all or most of the burials in the Turner cemetery, but only if the estimate of years of occupancy of a structure is increased to five. The estimate of the number of occupants per structure could be increased from the preferred figure of five to six, but the average structure size at Snodgrass (236 ft.^{2}) is considerably smaller than that at Turner, so that this alternative seems less desirable than the first. These results are only suggestive; it can not be stated that the people of Snodgrass were buried at Turner, only that it seems likely. It is possible that individuals from nearby hamlets such as

TABLE 35 Man-Years for Turner and Snodgrass Derived from Cook and Heizer's Approach

Site	*Population*	*Years of Occupancy*	
		2.5	*5.0*
Turner	310	775	1550
Snodgrass	626	1565	3130
Total	936	2340	4680

TABLE 36 Man-Years for Turner and Snodgrass Derived from the Structure/Number Approach

Years of Occupancy	*Occupants Per Structure*					
	3	*4*	*5*	*6*	*7*	*8*
2.5	975	1300	1625	1950	2275	2600
5.0	1950	2600	3250	3900	4550	5200

Stick Chimney were also buried at Turner. At present, since there is no means to test these hypotheses, the knowledge that the Turner cemetery served more than the resident population must suffice.

Social Organization

The data from the Turner cemetery will now be used in an attempt to elucidate certain aspects of the social organization of the group or groups burying their dead at Turner. It will be assumed that culture is a system, and that the variability of this system may be explained in terms of its interactions with other systems. It is further assumed that people who are treated differentially in life will be treated differentially in death.

The social organization of Middle Mississippian societies, such as the Powers phase, has been considered by several writers. Middle Mississippian societies have been variously characterized as states (Sears 1968), as ranked societies (Brown 1971, Peebles 1971, 1974), and as possessed of a well-developed class system with hereditary chiefs (Griffin 1967). It has been suggested that smaller sites, such as Turner, functioning within a larger ranked system will appear egalitarian in their organization (Goldstein 1976). These alternative forms of social organization will be evaluated for the Turner site with data from the cemetery. First, however, the state level of social organization may be ruled out.

Peebles (1974) rejected, on the basis of logical and historical considerations, the hypothesis proposed by Sears (1968) that Mississippian societies were states. It is assumed, therefore, that the Turner site participated in either an egalitarian or a ranked society.

A number of studies have been made of mortuary practices at other Mississippian sites and phases for the information these practices provide on social organization. The results of these studies can be summarized briefly. When the study has focused on a large ceremonial center, the results have indicated a ranked society (Brown 1971, Peebles 1974). When the study has focused on smaller sites in isolation from ceremonial centers, the results have indicated egalitarian societies (Goldstein 1976). When, however, the study has focused on small sites in conjunction with their ceremonial center, evidence for the participation of the small sites in a ranked society has been detected (Peebles 1971). As the results of studies on other small Mississippian cemeteries may have relevance to the present investigation, these studies merit lengthier discussion.

In her analysis of data from the small Mississippian cemeteries from the Moss and Schild sites, Goldstein tested the hypothesis that "the social organization of outlying Mississippian mortuary sites should appear essentially egalitarian" (1976:122). The results of the monothetic divisive clustering procedure she employed to determine the disposal types at the Moss and Schild sites appear to confirm this hypothesis.

Peeble's analyses of the Moundville phase sites began with the examination of several small cemeteries–Koger's Island, Snow's Bend, Little Bear Creek, Flint River, and the Perry site. The analyses of Koger's Island and Snow's Bend have particular bearing on the summary statements made earlier concerning small Mississippian cemeteries.

At Koger's Island, Peebles (1971) noted that burials bearing certain classes of socio-technic grave goods were spatially segregated from the remainder of the cemetery. This segregation of artifact classes demonstrates a differentiation of status and might be indicative of the participation of the Koger's Island people in a ranked society. However, that a few individuals were given more elaborate grave goods than others does not necessarily mean that they were of higher rank. In an egalitarian society, some people are wealthier than others or enjoy a higher status because of their personal achievements. If personal achievement is reflected in the burial treatment of the dead, then a few comparatively wealthy burials are expected in the cemetery of an egalitarian group. Koger's Island could be an example of just such a situation. Certain of the socio-technic goods which were segregated in the burials at Koger's Island were associated exclusively with adult males and therefore appear to be related to age, sex, and possibly achievement.

Several lines of evidence indicated that the Koger's Island population interacted with the ranked society at Moundville (Peebles 1971:71-78). If, however, the Moundville material had not been available for comparison, the Koger's Island cemetery would not have been recognized as the remains of a segment of a ranked society. Koger's Island represents an essentially egalitarian population participating in the Moundville ranked society at a low level.

The results of Peebles's (1971) study of a small Moundville phase cemetery from Snow's Bend reinforce the suggestions made above. Virtually none of the items Peebles considered to be indicative of status or rank were recovered during the partial excavation of the Snow's Bend cemetery (DeJarnette and Peebles 1970). None of the local symbols common to other Moundville phase sites were found there, and the only supra-local symbols were engraved or incised on pottery vessels. Because of the lack of these critical socio-technic items, no evidence for anything but an egalitarian system could be recognized. A test did show that the areal distribution of burials with and without grave goods was non-random, but it is difficult to interpret this as evidence for ranking. Peebles (1974:74) has suggested that sampling error is responsible for the dearth of local and supra-local symbols, since only 47 burials were excavated. Yet, it seems quite possible that the burials already excavated are representative of the cemetery, and that no local or supra-local artifacts or local symbols are present at Snow's Bend. Snow's Bend probably represents another basically egalitarian local group participating in the Moundville system. It could also be that the egalitarian appearance of the Snow's Bend cemetery is due to the site's proximity to Moundville. Even if an individual of a ranking lineage had lived and died at Snow's Bend, his remains could easily have been removed to Moundville for interment.

At Moundville, the situation with respect to ranking is clear. Peebles (1974) demonstrated that the Moundville population was organized into two main classes. Individuals in the lower class were distinguished in death on the bases of age, sex, and achievement. Those in the upper class were also distinguished by an ascriptive element which cross-cut age and sex distinctions. Individuals in the upper rank were buried separately from the remainder of the population and were accompanied by different classes of offerings. The distinctions which were made were repeated and systematic, and clearly could not be attributed to an egalitarian society. Yet, if only the village burials (as opposed to cemeteries near the mounds) had been excavated at Moundville, the sample would have included only low rank burials, and the society might have appeared egalitarian.

The examples of Snow's Bend and Koger's Island demonstrate the importance of sampling the mortuary practices of an entire society rather than a segment of a society. When these sites are considered in isolation, they appear to represent the remains of egalitarian populations. Yet, when they are considered together with their ceremonial center, it can be seen that they participated in a ranked society.

From the preceding discussion it is evident that only under rare circumstances will the study of the mortuary practices of a segment of a society provide indications of ranked social organization. It is proposed here that the Turner site represents only a segment of the total Powers phase society, and that the Turner cemetery will appear to be that of an egalitarian group or groups. The burial data will be examined for any structuring related to age, sex, burial form, orientation, number of individuals per burial, and burial accompaniments. This evidence will then be used to refute or substantiate the proposition.

The data to be used in the examination of the structure of the Turner cemetery are presented in Appendix E. These data are also summarized in a series of one-way tables (Tables 37-42). Burials 6, 10, and 11 are omitted because the information available for them is too scanty. Burials 54 and 58 are not included because it is unlikely that they were prehistoric features.

A series of cross-tabulations was made and tested to see whether any significant associations could be found among burial form, individual age and sex, orientation, and the number of individuals per burial. The cross-tabula-

TABLE 37 Tabulation of Age

Child (1 - 15)	22
Adult (15+)	77
Unknown age	3
Total	102

TABLE 38 Tablulation of Sex (Adults Only)

Male	22
Female	46
Indeterminate	9
Total	77

TABLE 39 Tabulation of Form

Form	*All Cases*	*Certain*	*Probable*	*Uncertain*
Articulated	58	42	16	0
Partly articulated	1	1	0	0
Bundle	20	18	2	0
Single skull	15	5	9	1
Unknown	8	0	0	8
Total	102	66	27	9

TABLE 40 Tabulation of Position

Extended supine	57
Disarticulated	43
Other	2
Total	102

TABLE 41 Tabulation of Orientation

E	7
ESE	39
SE	3
W	5
WNW	4
NW	1

TABLE 42 Number of Individuals Per Burial

Number	*Cases*	*Total*
1	27	27
2	10	20
3	5	15
4	5	20
5	4	20
Total	51	102

tions were tested for significance with the G-statistic (Sokal and Rohlf 1969). *G* is approximately distributed as chi-square and may be tested against the critical values found in a table of chi-square values.

The first three-way test was Form vs. Single/Multiple vs. Age (Table 43). Burial form was divided into four classes: articulated, partly articulated, bundle, and single skull. Single/Multiple (Sinmul) was a binary variable which separated the single burials from the various multiple burials. Age was a variable with two classes: child (1.5 to 15 years), and adult (15 years and older). The cross-tabulation was further partitioned by a variable (Cert) which represented my assessment of the certainty of the form of the burial. In many extended supine burials, the epiphyses of the long bones were gone, but the bones were properly arranged to represent the remains of an articulated burial. In cases such as this, form was considered definite, and the variable Cert was scored as "Def." In a few instances, however, pothunters had so disturbed the burial that the reliability of any statement about form was questionable. In cases such as these, form was uncertain, and depending on the degree of disturbance, Cert was scored as "probable" or as "missing data." Another example of this is the single skull burials of children. Because preservation was poor and since small soft bones might easily be overlooked or troweled away, most of these burials were scored as "probable" or "missing data" on the certainty variable.

The results of the Form by Sinmul by Age analysis showed that Form could not be considered independent of either of the other two variables. Age was independent of Sinmul, and there was no interaction among the three variables. Furthermore, the three variables were not jointly independent, due mainly to the relationship of Form with the other two variables. The main cause of the significant results was the bundle burials. The bundle burials occurred only in multiple burials and included only adults. The single skull burials did not appear to vary significantly here, but if all burials had been considered, not just those for which form was certain, then they would have

TABLE 43 A Three-Way Cross-Tabulation of Form, Age, and Multiplicity of Burial (Includes Only Those Cases for Which Form is Certain)

		Sinmul		
Form	*Age*	*Single*	*Multiple*	*Total*
Articulated	Child	3	2	5
	Adult	13	24	37
	Total	16	26	42
Partly articulated	Child	0	0	0
	Adult	1	0	1
	Total	1	0	1
Bundle	Child	0	0	0
	Adult	0	15	15
	Total	0	15	15
Single skull	Child	0	3	3
	Adult	0	2	2
	Total	0	5	5

Summary of Analysis

Hypothesis Tested	*DF*	*G*	*Significance*
Form by Sinmul independence	3	17.6504	.001
Form by Age independence	3	10.5654	.025
Age by Sinmul independence	1	.4856	NS
Form by Sinmul by Age interaction	3	.6318	NS
Form by Sinmul by Age independence	10	29.3332	.005

contributed to the variability. Thirteen child skulls may have been buried without post-cranial remains, although this is certain for only three, while only two adults were buried in this fashion.

The partitioning variable "Cert=Def" was used for the 3-way cross-tabulation, but wasn't really necessary for the 2-way cross-tabulation of Age and Sinmul (Table 44). When all cases were used, the sample size was increased from 63 to 99. Age and Sinmul were still independent for the larger sample.

A second three-way cross-tabulation was analyzed for the variables Form, Persons, and Age, once again partitioned by "Cert=Def" (Table 45). The variable Persons was the same as Sinmul, except that it did not collapse burials containing two to five people into one multiple class, but instead retained each burial size as a categorical variable. In this way, a test could be made for significant differences among the multiple burials. After examining the table, though, it was evident that there was little difference among the multiple burials, other than the number of individuals. No significant inter-

TABLE 44 A Two-Way Cross-Tabulation of Age and Multiplicity of Burial (Includes All Cases with Known Age)

	Sinmul		
Age	*Single*	*Multiple*	*Total*
Child	7	15	22
Adult	20	57	77
Total	27	72	99
G=.073	df=1	Not significant	

TABLE 45 A Three-Way Cross-Tabulation of Form, Age and the Number of Individuals Per Burial (Includes Only Those Cases for Which Form is Certain)

		Persons					
Form	*Age*	*1*	*2*	*3*	*4*	*5*	*Total*
Articulated	Child	3	1	1	0	0	5
	Adult	13	7	5	9	3	37
	Total	16	8	6	9	3	42
Partly articulated	Child	0	0	0	0	0	0
	Adult	1	0	0	0	0	1
	Total	1	0	0	0	0	1
Bundle	Child	0	0	0	0	0	0
	Adult	0	4	4	6	1	15
	Total	0	4	4	6	1	15
Single skull	Child	0	1	1	0	1	3
	Adult	0	0	1	1	0	2
	Total	0	1	2	1	1	5

Summary of Analysis

Hypothesis Tested	*DF*	*G*	*Significance*
Form by Persons independence	12	19.3548	NS
Form by Age independence	3	10.5654	.025
Age by Persons independence	4	5.1350	NS
Form by Persons by Age interaction	12	2.6066	NS
Form by Persons by Age independence	31	37.6618	NS

actions between variables were discovered, other than the one between Form and Age which was noted in the previous three-way analysis. The effect of replacing the variable Sinmul with Persons has been to mask the relationship of form with burial size. Age and Persons were found to be independent.

However, the sample size for this test could be legitimately increased by omitting the unnecessary partitioning variable Cert. Even with the larger sample size, Age and Persons were still unrelated (Table 46).

The third three-way cross-tabulation used the variables Form, Persons, and Sex partitioned by "Cert=Def" (Table 47). The sample size was reduced to 50 by the exclusion of children. The variables were mutually independent, whether considered simultaneously or as pairs. The sample size for the Form

TABLE 46 A Two-Way Cross-Tabulation of Age and the Number of Persons in a Burial (Includes All Cases with Known Age)

	Persons					
Age	*1*	*2*	*3*	*4*	*5*	*Total*
Child	7	4	3	3	5	22
Adult	15	16	10	17	14	77
Total	22	20	13	20	19	99

G=1.1082 df=4 Not significant

TABLE 47 A Three-Way Cross-Tabulation of Form, Sex, and the Number of Persons in a Burial (Includes Only Adults of Known Sex for Whom Form is Certain)

		Persons					
Form	*Sex*	*1*	*2*	*3*	*4*	*5*	*Total*
Articulated	Male	5	1	3	2	0	11
	Female	8	6	2	7	3	26
	Total	13	7	5	9	3	37
Partly articulated	Male	0	0	0	0	0	0
	Female	1	0	0	0	0	1
	Total	1	0	0	0	0	1
Bundle	Male	0	1	1	1	0	3
	Female	0	3	2	4	0	9
	Total	0	4	3	5	0	12

Summary of Analysis

Hypothesis Tested	*DF*	*G*	*Significance*
Form by Persons independence	8	13.8968	NS
Form by Sex independence	2	.7658	NS
Sex by Persons independence	4	4.9766	NS
Form by Persons by Sex interaction	8	.9016	NS
Form by Persons by Sex independence	22	20.5408	NS

by Persons two-way table could be increased by adding the five unsexed individuals of known form, but the result was still not significant. However, when the table was collapsed to Form by Sinmul, the result was highly significant (Table 48). The *G*-score itself did not change much, but the degrees of freedom dropped from 12 to 3. The significant result was due to the exclusive occurrence of bundles in multiple burials. The variables Sex and Persons were examined in a two-way table without the partitioning variable "Cert=Def." This increased the sample size to 68, but the result was still not significant (Table 49). The result was again not significant when Persons was collapsed into the two-class variable Sinmul (Table 50).

The distinctions discovered in the three-way cross-tabulations may be quickly summarized. Burial form is related to age: only adults were buried as bundles, and, with two exceptions, only children were buried as single skulls. Burial form is also related to the number of people in a burial, because bundle burials occurred only in multiple burials. This last is true for adults and children, and for adults alone. Age is unrelated to the number of persons in a burial, and sex is unrelated to form or the number of persons.

TABLE 48 A Two-Way Cross-Tabulation of Form and Multiplicity of Burial (Includes All Adults for Whom Burial Form is Certain)

Form	*Sinmul* *Single*	*Multiple*	*Total*
Articulated	13	24	37
Partly articulated	1	0	1
Bundle	0	15	15
Single skull	0	2	2
Total	14	41	55

G=14.3474 df=3 p<.01

TABLE 49 A Two-Way Cross-Tabulation of Sex and the Number of Persons in a Burial (Includes All Adults of Known Sex)

Sex	*Persons* *1*	*2*	*3*	*4*	*5*	*Total*
Male	6	4	4	3	5	22
Female	11	12	4	11	8	46
Total	17	16	8	14	13	68

G=2.5814 df=3 Not significant

TABLE 50 A Two-Way Cross-Tabulation of Sex and the Multiplicity of Burial (Includes All Adults of Known Sex)

Sex	*Sinmul*		
	Single	*Multiple*	*Total*
Male	6	16	22
Female	11	35	46
Total	17	51	68
G=.3518	df=1	Not significant	

Two-way tables were constructed to test Orientation against Age and Sex. Although Orientation was initially scored as a categorical variable with 16 classes (e.g., N, NNE, NE, ENE, E, etc.), it was reduced to two classes for the purposes of these tests. There were two main reasons for this. First, in a disturbed skeleton, it was often difficult to distinguish the exact orientation, yet a choice had to be made between west and west-northwest, for example. Second, the sample divided quite clearly into two classes: one with heads to the east (from E to SE), and another with the heads to the west (W to NW). Analyses of the two-way tables showed that Age and Sex were both independent of the orientation of the individual (Tables 51 and 52).

TABLE 51 A Two-Way Cross-Tabulation of Age and Orientation (Includes All Articulated and Partly Articulated Burials)

Age	*Orientation*		
	East	*West*	*Total*
Child	7	0	7
Adult	42	10	52
Total	49	10	59
G=.6500	df=1	Not significant	

To test the hypothesis of assortative burying of adults and children, expected frequencies of the various combinations were calculated assuming random combinations of individuals with respect to age. For this test, a total of 94 individuals of known ages in 49 burials could be used. Other burials included individuals of unknown age and were omitted from the test. Of the 94 individuals, 22 were children (under age 15) and 72 were adults. Twenty-seven people were buried alone, while there were ten double, four triple, five quadruple, and three quintuple burials.

TABLE 52 A Two-Way Cross-Tabulation of Sex and Orientation (Includes All Articulated and Partly Articulated Burials of Adults of Known Sex)

	Orientation		
Sex	*East*	*West*	*Total*
Male	13	2	15
Female	26	7	33
Total	39	9	48

G=.0630 df=1 Not significant

A binomial expansion was used to calculate the expected probability of each event in each table. For example, the probability of a triple burial containing three children was calculated as follows. The probability of any given individual in a burial being a child was .234 (22/94). Therefore, the probability of all three individuals in a triple burial being children was $.234^3=.013$. Similarly, the probability of a triple burial containing only adults was $.766^3=.449$. The remaining kinds of triple burials included both adults and children, and their probability of occurrence was *1-.013=.449=.538*. The expected frequency of burials of each type could then be computed by multiplying the observed number of triple burials (4) by each probability. The expected probabilities and frequencies for the various combinations of adults and children for the different burial sizes are shown in Table 53. The observed frequencies are compared to the expected frequencies in Table 54.

The observed frequencies are in every case very close to the expected frequencies. The fit for burial size=5 would be even closer had B-13 been included. Burial 13 had four adults and one individual of unknown age, who could not be located in the lab. In the field notes, this individual was sexed, which means it was probably an adult. If it were, the observed proportion for "mixed" would be .75, which is virtually identical to the expected .736.

In the next two tests, only individuals of known sex and juveniles were included. Because these constraints would have reduced the sample size a great deal, it was decided to include burials with individuals of unknown sex. However, the individuals of unknown sex were themselves omitted. Thus, Burial 13 which comprised five individuals (three females, one adult of unknown sex, and one individual of unknown age) was treated as a triple burial of three females. The first question examined using these data was assortative burial of adults on the basis of sex. The expected probabilities and frequencies were computed from the observed proportions of males (23/70=.329) and females (47/70=.671) in the burials to be tested. The

TABLE 53 Expected Frequencies and Probabilities of Exclusive and Mixed Burials of Children and Adults in Different Size Burials

Burial Size	*N*		*Burial Composition* Child Only	Adult Only	Mixed
1	27	Freq	6.3	20.7	0
		Prob	0.234	0.766	0
2	10	Freq	0.6	5.9	3.6
		Prob	0.055	0.587	0.358
3	4	Freq	0	1.8	2.2
		Prob	0.013	0.449	0.538
4	5	Freq	0	1.7	3.3
		Prob	0.003	0.344	0.653
5	3	Freq	0	0.8	2.2
		Prob	0.0007	0.264	0.736

TABLE 54 Observed and Expected Frequencies of Exclusive and Mixed Burials of Children and Adults in Different Size Burials

Burial Size	*N*		*Burial Composition* Child Only	Adult Only	Mixed
1	27	Observed	7	20	0
		Expected	6.3	20.7	0
2	10	Observed	0	6	4
		Expected	0.6	5.9	3.6
3	4	Observed	0	1	3
		Expected	0	1.8	2.2
4	5	Observed	0	2	3
		Expected	0	1.7	3.3
5	3	Observed	0	0	3
		Expected	0	0.8	2.2

expected probabilities and frequencies and the observed frequencies are shown in Table 55.

The fit is good, except where the number of sexed individuals is two. There is slight excess of mixed sex burials and a slight deficit of paired female burials. It is not a very large difference, and it does not seem particularly significant. Had the imbalance been such that there were only mixed sex double burials and no double male or double female burials, there might be a basis for suspecting a deliberate cultural practice.

The third and final question examined was whether children were preferentially buried with adult males or females. A table very similar to Table 55 was set up, the difference being that only multiple burials including children were tabulated. The results are shown in Table 56. The only notable deviation is the burial of a child with two males. This is Burial 33, and the field notes suggest that the child may not actually have been part of that burial, but a later intrusion. The case of a child with a single adult male is from triple Burial 22 where one adult is unsexed. Thus, there might be a slight tendency for a child in a double burial to be interred with an adult female. The small sample size prevents any truly definitive statements here.

TABLE 55 Test for Assortative Burial on the Basis of Sex

Number of Sexed Adults in Burial	N	Burial Composition: Males Only	Females Only	Mixed
1	22	7.2 (.329) 7	14.8 (.671) 15	
2	8	0.9 (.108) 1	3.6 (.451) 2	3.5 (.441) 5
3	8	0.3 (.035) 0	2.4 (.303) 3	5.3 (.662) 5
4	2	0 (.012) 0	0.4 (.203) 1	1.6 (.785) 1

Note: The first figure in each cell is the expected frequency, the second (in parentheses) is the expected probability, and the third is the observed frequency.

TABLE 56 Test for Assortative Burial of Children with Adult Males or Females

Number of Sexed Adults in Burial	N	Burial Composition: Males Only	Females Only	Mixed Sexes
1	5	1.6 (.329) 1	3.4 (.671) 4	
2	2	0.2 (.108) 1	0.9 (.451) 0	0.9 (.441) 1
3	5	0.2 (.035) 0	1.5 (.303) 1	3.3 (.662) 4
4	1	0 (.012) 0	0.2 (.203) 0	0.8 (.785) 1

Note: The first figure in each cell is the expected frequency, the second (in parentheses) is the expected probability, and the third is the observed frequency.

The combined results of the three tests appear to show that there is no evidence for assortative burial of children or adults of either sex. Apparently, no attempt was made to separate the burials by age or sex.

The cemetery was examined to see if there was any spatial segregation on the bases of age and sex. No patterns of segregation could be discerned. Furthermore, multiple and bundle burials appeared to be evenly distributed throughout the cemetery. That is, no row of the cemetery could be singled out as a "bundle" row or an all male row.

So far, the analyses have not considered the artifacts placed with the burials. It is apparent that the composition of the pottery assemblage differs between the burials and the Turner and Snodgrass villages (Table 57). More bottles occurred in the cemetery than in the village refuse, and the only long neck bottles were found with burials. The frequency of effigy bowls in the cemetery was also slightly higher. The frequencies of small jars and bowls were similar for the cemetery and the villages, but no large bowls or large jars occurred with burials. Thus, there was some selectivity regarding which pottery types were included in burials.

Unfortunately, little can be gained from a lengthy discussion of the associ-

TABLE 57 Whole Vessel Assemblages*

	Turner Village		*Snodgrass Village*		*Turner Cemetery*	
	No.	*%*	*No.*	*%*	*No.*	*%*
Undecorated jars						
Small	8	18	3	4	5	12
Large	11	24	19	26	0	0
Undecorated bowls						
Small	7	16	13	18	8	19
Large	5	11	9	12	0	0
Short neck bottles	4	9	8	11	13	31 (1 dec.)
Long neck bottles	0	0	0	0	6	14
Effigy bowls	1	2	8	11	8	19
Other	3	7	3	4	1	2
Decorated jars						
Small	0	0	3	4	0	0
Large	0	0	1	1	0	0
Decorated bowls						
Small	4	9	2	3	0	0
Large	0	0	1	1	0	0
Total	45#		72#		42†	

*James E. Price, ms in author's possession
#Includes 2 vessels of unknown size
†Includes 1 vessel of unknown size

ations of individuals with artifact classes. Many of the burials were badly disturbed, and their grave goods were stolen. For some burials, a partial inventory is available, and from this a few gross generalizations can be made. Information regarding the artifacts found with the burials and the state of the burials when excavated is presented in Table 58. If this list is used in conjunction with the Turner cemetery map, it can be seen that the pothunters' activities were restricted primarily to the central portion of the cemetery. Few pots escaped detection there, and those were in poor condition. On the periphery of the cemetery, several burials remained undisturbed and retained their accompaniments.

Although few undisturbed burials remained for the archaeologists to excavate, it appears that the main distinctions in terms of the goods occurring with burials are distinctions of quantity, not kind. For example, of the undisturbed burials which were excavated, many had no pottery, a few had one pot, one had two pots, and another had three. If the reports of the pothunters are credible, one double burial had 11 pots in it. Only 42 pots are known to have been removed from the cemetery, so if 11 were in one burial, a few of the disturbed burials may have been without pots. The overall appearance is of individuals buried with only one or two pots, if any, with a single possible exception.

It is now in order to look at the associations of pottery with individuals of known age and sex. Where they can be assigned to a particular individual, the pots were found with females in six cases, juveniles in two cases, a male in one case, and an adult of unknown sex in another case. The sample size is so small that it is not possible to recognize any meaningful divisions on the basis of age or sex. However, the infant burials were separated from the adults by the exclusive inclusion with infants of large (usually over 100 cm^2) sherds. Thus, the infants, already separated from the adults on the basis of burial location, were further separated by another attribute.

There is a very notable break in artifact associations with burial form. It is evident that no artifacts were intentionally buried with bundle burials. None of the pots recovered could be definitely associated with a bundle, and the few artifacts which were found with bundles could either have been incidental inclusions or could have belonged to other individuals in the same grave. In this respect, it is interesting to note that Burial 8 from Snodgrass had apparently been disinterred for reburial, with only a few pieces of bone remaining behind. Also left behind were all the artifacts included in the original burial. What this may represent, then, is a portion of a burial program in which an individual was buried with such goods as were appropriate. At a later date, the major part of his skeleton was exhumed and reburied as a bundle with another individual. So far, B-8 from Snodgrass is the only

TABLE 58 Powers Phase Burials: Artifact Distribution and Record of Disturbance

Site	*Burial Number*	*Disturbance**	*Pots Remaining#*	*Other Artifacts*
23BU10	1	P	1	none
	2	P	1	5 Scallorn points, 4 flint chips, 2 crystal artifacts, 1 antler flaking tool, 1 pebble hammerstone, 1 bone fishhook, 1 scraper
	3A	P	-	2 points, turtle carapace (knee rattle?)
	3B	P	-	none
	5	P	1	none
	6	P	-	none
	STR 1 B-1	-	-	none
	STR 1 B-2	-	-	none
	STR 1 B-3	-	-	sherd, rodent jaw (from disturbance?)
23BU21B	1	+	?	none
	2	?	?	none
	3	?	1	deer mandible and maxilla (?)
	4A	-	-	gypsum
	4B	-	-	large rim sherd
	7	P	2	deer bone
	8	-	1	2 pieces of galena, 1 ear plug, 1 quartz crystal, 1 deer skull, some hematite
	STR 19 B-1	?	?	?
	STR 19 burned	-	-	none (disturbed aboriginally)
	STR 20 B-1	?	?	?
	STR 42 B-1	-	-	2 large jar sherds, shell
	STR 42 B-2	-	-	large bowl rim, large body sherd, 2 flakes
	STR 44 B-1	-	1	none
	STR 45 B-1	-	-	hammerstone, concretion, sherd clay lump (disturbed aboriginally, may not be Powers phase burial)
	STR 47 B-1	-	-	tiny jar made from leg of tripodal vessel, deer tooth
	STR 48 B-1	-	-	large body sherd
	STR 50 B-1	-	-	none
	STR 77 B-1	-	-	large body sherd
23BU21A	1	-	-	none
	2	+	0	Archaic projectile point
	3	-	-	none
	4	+	0	none

TABLE 58, cont.

Site	Burial Number	Disturbance	Pots Remaining	Other Artifacts
23BU21A (cont.)				
	5 (all)	–	1	none
	6 (all)	+,P	?	none
	7	–	–	deer effigy broken off a pot (probably unintentional)
	8A	+	0	2 deer ulna awls, beaver tooth gouge, 3 projectile points
	8B,C,D	+	0	none
	10	?	?	?
	11	?	?	?
	12 (both)	+	1	none
	13A	–	–	knee rattle
	13B	–	2	projectile point
	13A&B	–	–	share a tool kit
	13C	–	1	bear claw, shell
	13D&E	–	–	none
	14	–	2	none
	15	+	–	none
	16 (both)	–	–	none
	18 (all)	+	0	none
	19A	–	2	none
	19B	–	–	none
	20	+	–	charred corn
	21 (both)	+	0	none
	22 (all)	–	–	none
	23	+	0	none
	24 (all)	+	0	none
	25 (both)	–	–	none
	26	+	0	none
	27	?	?	none
	28 (all)	–	–	bone needle
	29	–	–	celt
	30	–	–	none
	31 (all)	+	0	none
	32	+	0	none
	33 (all)	–	–	none
	34	+	1	3 shells, 3 hammerstones, celt
	35A	–	–	knife
	35B	–	1	base of stemmed point
	35C&D	–	–	none
	36 (both)	+	0	supposedly had 11 pots
	37 (both)	+	0	none
	38A,B,C,D	+	0	none
	38E	+	1	projectile point, creek rock
	39	?	?	none

TABLE 58, cont.

Site	*Burial Number*	*Disturbance*	*Pots Remaining*	*Other Artifacts*
23BU21A (cont.)				
	40	+	0	none
	41 (both)	+	0	none
	43	+,P	?	none
	44	+	1	none
	45	+	0	raccoon maxilla fragment (possibly unintentional)
	46	+	0	arrowshaft abrader, worked chert
	47	+	0	none
	48	+	0	none
	49	+	0	none
	51	P	–	none
	52 (all)	+	0	Scallorn point
	53 (both)	?	?	bone needle
	55 (all)	+	0	Scallorn point, antlers, small hammerstone
	56	+	0	Archaic point (in rodent burrow)
	57	?	?	none
	59	–	–	none
	60	+	1	none
	STR 27 B-1	–	1	none

*A "+" means that pothunters disturbed the burial, a "P" means that plowing damaged the burial, a "–" means that the burial was undisturbed, and a "?" means that information is too scanty for any decision.
#A number indicates the number of pots left; a "–" means that pots were probably never present; and a "?" indicates that no pots were recovered, but whether this was the burial's original condition or the result of looting is uncertain.

apparent example of this practice, although STR 45 B-1 from that site may be another case of the same practice.

The distributions of non-ceramic artifacts appear random. The artifacts chosen for burial were almost all utilitarian, and their associations with particular individuals seem idiosyncratic. For example, only one burial has a beaver tooth gouge, only one has antlers, and only one has a bear claw. Few artifact types appeared more than once, and those that did appear more often were not assigned to a particular age or sex class. For instance, of the eight burials with associated projectile points, one was a male, three were females, none was a juvenile, and four were individuals of unknown age or sex, or were not definitely associated with the points. None of the artifacts excavated by the archaeologists could be considered a supra-local artifact or symbol, and no socio-technic items occurred with sufficient frequency to be recognized as local symbols or artifacts. The looters did not find any of the artifacts they had hoped for; there were no monolithic axes, no cache blades, no elaborate pottery vessels, no copper artifacts. Admittedly, the techniques used to recover most of the artifacts from the cemetery were atrocious and record-keeping was inadequate, but from the information that has been collected, it can be surmised that the loss was not so serious as it seemed at first. To the best of my knowledge, the archaeologists obtained a sample of every artifact class present in the cemetery, even if it was a small sample.

What are the implications of all the preceding analyses for social organization in the Powers phase? The proposition being tested here is that the Turner cemetery appears egalitarian. In an egalitarian society, the differences in social personae should be ranked along a continuum, with the distinctions observable determined only by age, sex, and achievement. A ranked society will also differentiate many individual social personae on these same bases of age and sex, but there will also be an ascribed dimension cross-cutting them. Age and sex distinctions may be minimized in the upper ranks, but will remain important in the lower ranks.

So far, no sex-based differences in burial treatment have been noticed. The only age distinctions are related to form, burial location, and artifacts accompanying the burial. Burial form has also been related to the number of individuals in the grave, but to nothing else. Although the archaeologists did not excavate all the artifacts, they were able to observe the collections of the pothunters, and nothing unique or truly different was found in those collections. The only differences in the goods buried with individuals were differences of quantity, not kind. Nothing was found to parallel either the supra-local or local symbols which Peebles (1971) found in his examination of Moundville phase sites. No cross-cutting distinctions were found that would clearly separate one part of the cemetery population from another. There was inadequate evidence to test for spatial segregation on the basis of the possession of grave goods, because the cemetery had been looted. In sum, no evidence for a ranked society has been found using the information available from the Turner cemetery. The proposition that the Turner cemetery appears egalitarian cannot be rejected. This does not mean that the Powers phase was not a ranked society, merely that ranking was not reflected in the limited class of remains from the Turner cemetery that could be used for analysis. These results may mean that if the Powers phase was a ranked society, then no one from the ranking lineage lived at Turner, or that those who did were returned to Powers Fort for burial when they died.

5

Conclusions and Substantive Contributions

The single most important result of this investigation is the demonstration that the analysis of poorly preserved human skeletal remains is not only feasible but fruitful. As part of the research for this paper, a new means of sexing fragmentary human bones has been developed and utilized. Had the usual means of determining sex been practical, it is quite likely that femoral circumference would never have been used as a means for identifying sex. Furthermore, had the long bones been intact, the errors in Steele and McKern's (1969) regression equations for predicting long bone length would have gone unnoticed.

Another contribution to physical anthropology has been documentation (for one population) of the relationship between calculus deposits and periodontal disease. Age has been shown to be significantly related to alveolar resorption and general dental pathology. Attention has also been drawn to the masking effect that antemortem tooth loss has on statistics related to tooth disease. Any comparisons of dental pathology between populations must take these relationships and effects into consideration or risk being misleading or inaccurate.

The data from the age analyses were used in the construction of a life table for the individuals buried in the Turner cemetery. A series of assumptions was made in order to relate the Turner life table to a more biologically realistic life table (Weiss 1973). This life table was then used to demonstrate that the Turner cemetery was either used longer than Turner was occupied, or was used by more people than inhabited the Turner site.

Finally, it was argued that minor Mississippian cemeteries would appear to represent the mortuary practices of an egalitarian population. The Turner cemetery was used as a test of this proposition and appeared to substantiate the argument.

A brief sketch of the life of a Powers phase villager can be presented, based on the information contained in this report.

The vast majority of the individuals buried at the Turner site were born elsewhere and lived most or all of their lives at other locations. This was demonstrated by the computations at the end of the Demography section of this paper.

Once a person was born, he had about 70 percent chance of surviving the first year of his life. If he died before he was one and a half or two years old (that is, before he was weaned), he was buried beneath the floor of the house he had lived in, and a large sherd was placed near his head.

Those who survived weaning were placed on a diet which had enough sugar to rot their teeth and enough grit to wear their teeth down slowly. If one of these people died before he attained his full growth, he was buried in the cemetery, alone or with others, as either an extended articulated burial or as a skull without associated postcranial remains. However, the probability of an individual dying between the ages of two and 15 or 20 was low compared to the probability of dying in infancy or after age 20. A person who survived to age 15 could expect 20 more years of life, which was about the same life expectancy that a neonate had.

If a person survived to age 35, he had probably been parent to three or four children, of whom one had died at an early age. By the age of 35, the adult had lived in a half-dozen different villages. It was the adults who were the usual but infrequent victims of violent death. Of the approximately 100 Powers phase adults examined, at least two males may have died from arrow wounds and one female may have been scalped.

The few adults who lived to be 60 had out-lived most of their friends and half of their children. Many of these aged individuals had very bad teeth, and some were partly crippled by arthritis. Their advanced age may have given them some status among their fellow villagers, but it did not entitle them to any special distinctions when they were interred at the Turner site. Perhaps the most important and distinguished inhabitants of the Powers phase villages were buried at Powers Fort; there certainly was no indication that anyone important was buried at Turner.

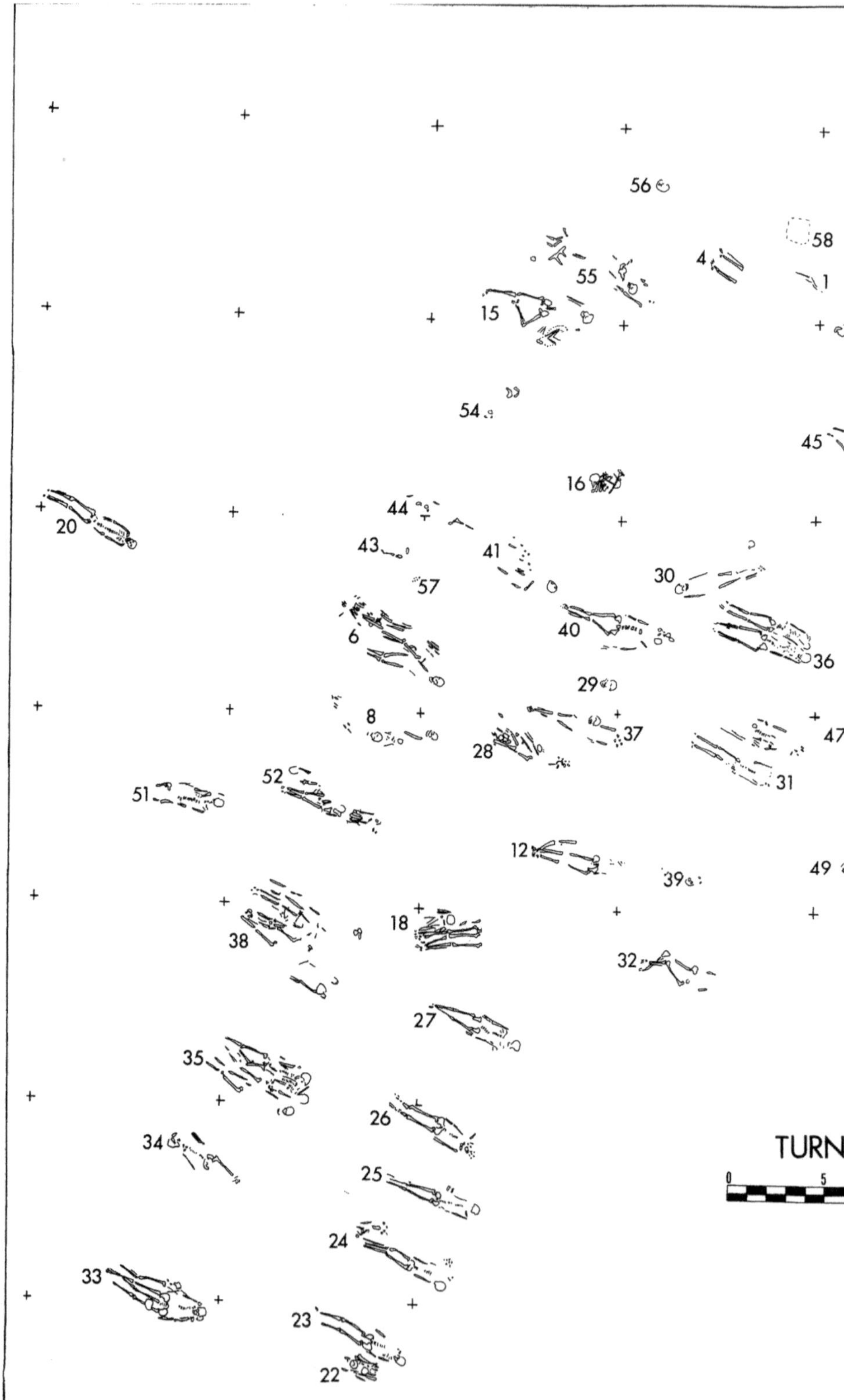

Figure 7. Turner Site Cemetery

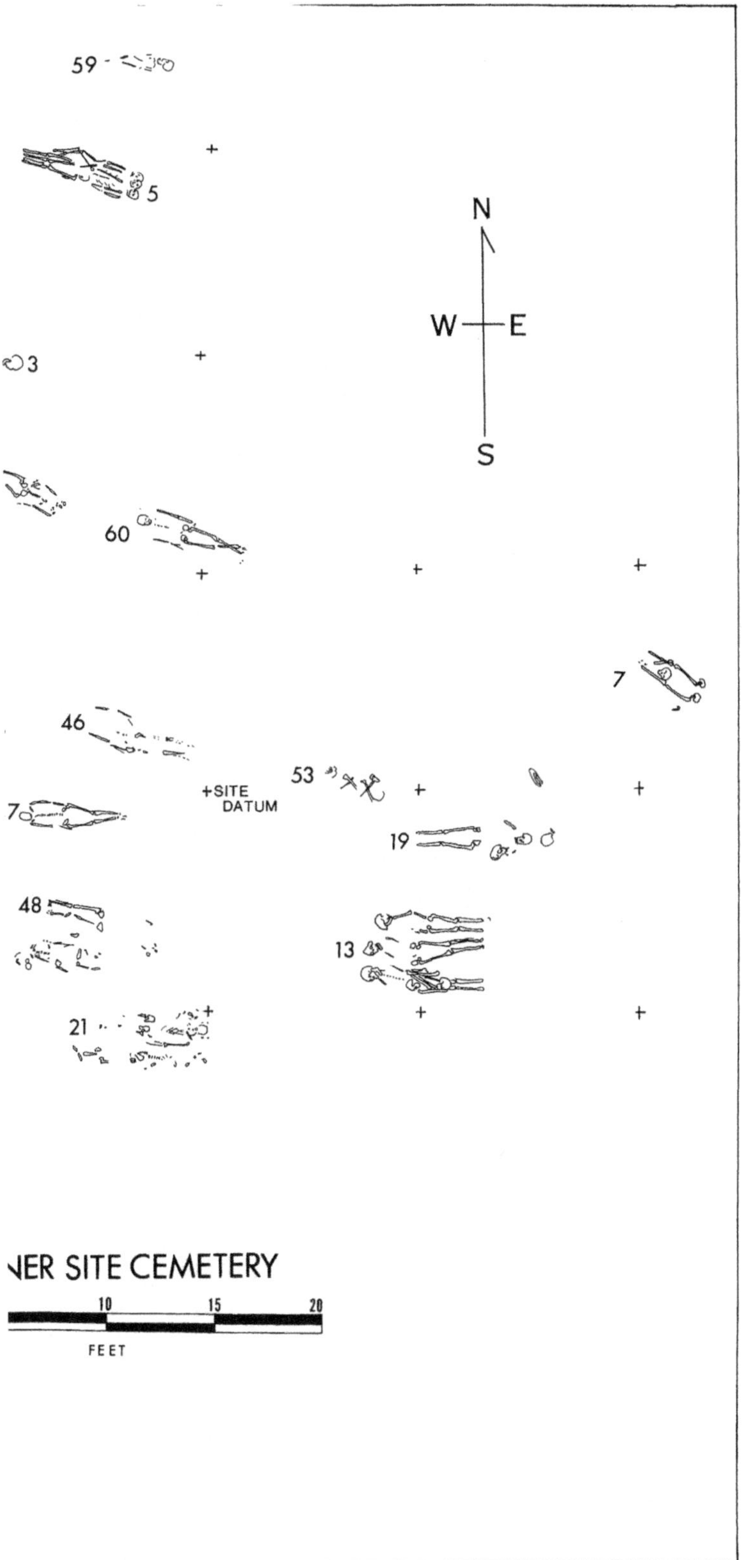
59
5
N
W
E
S
3
60
7
46
53
+SITE
DATUM
7
19
48
13
21
NER SITE CEMETERY
10
15
20
FEET

References Cited

Ahlqvist, J., and O. Damsten
1969 A Modification of Kerley's Method for the Microscopic Determinations of Age in Human Bones. Journal of Forensic Sciences 14:205-12.

Allison, M. J., D. Mendoza, and A. Pezzia
1974 A Radiographic Approach to Childhood Illness in Precolumbian Inhabitants of Southern Peru. American Journal of Physical Anthropology 40:409-16.

Anderson, James E.
1969 The Human Skeleton: A Manual for Archaeologists. Ottawa: The National Museums of Canada.

Asch, David L.
1973 A Middle Woodland Population Estimate for the Lower Illinois Valley. Unpublished manuscript, Museum of Anthropology, University of Michigan.

Bass, William M.
1971 Human Osteology: A Laboratory and Field Manual of the Human Skeleton. Columbia: Missouri Archaeological Society.

Bell, Robert E.
1960 Guide to the Identification of Certain American Indian Projectile Points. Oklahoma Anthropological Society, Special Bulletin 2.

Berry, A. Caroline, and R. J. Berry
1967 Epigenetic Variation in the Human Cranium. Journal of Anatomy 101:361-79.

Binford, Lewis R.
1964 Galley Pond Mound. In: Archaeological Investigations on Wassam Ridge, Southern Illinois University Museum. Archaeological Salvage Report 17.
1971 Mortuary Practices: Their Study and Potential. In: Approaches to the Social Dimensions of Mortuary Practices, edited by J. A. Brown. Society for American Archaeology, Memoir 25:6-29.

Birkby, Walter Hudson
1973 Discontinuous Morphological Traits of the Skull as Population Markers in the Prehistoric Southwest. Ph.D. Dissertation, University of Arizona, University Microfilms, Ann Arbor, Michigan.

Black, Thomas K., III
1972 A Comparison of the Settlement Patterns of the Turner and Snodgrass Sites. Unpublished manuscript, Museum of Anthropology, University of Michigan.
1973 Population Estimation from Burial Data of a Middle Mississippian Society. Unpublished manuscript, Museum of Anthropology, University of Michigan.
1978a A New Method for Assessing the Sex of Fragmentary Skeletal Remains: Femoral Shaft Circumference. American Journal of Physical Anthropology 48:227-31.

1978b A Method for Determining the Sex of Immature Human Skeletal Remains from Odontometric Dimensions. Ph.D. Dissertation, University of Michigan. University Microfilms, Ann Arbor, Michigan.

1979 The MMD and Population Distances. Paper presented at the meetings of the Society for American Archaeology. Vancouver, British Columbia.

Blakely, Robert L.

1971 Comparison of the Mortality Profiles of Archaic, Middle Woodland, and Middle Mississippian Skeletal Populations. American Journal of Physical Anthropology 34:43-54.

Blanco, R. A., R. M. Acheson, C. Canosa, and J. B. Salomon

1974 Height, Weight, and Lines of Arrested Growth in Young Guatemalan Children. American Journal of Physical Anthropology 40:39-48.

Brace, C. Loring, and Paul E. Mahler

1971 Post-Pleistocene Changes in the Human Dentition. American Journal of Physical Anthropology 34:191-204.

Brooks, S. T.

1955 Skeletal Age at Death: The Reliability of Cranial and Pubic Age Indicators. American Journal of Physical Anthropology, n.s. 13:567-98.

Brothwell, Don R.

1963 The Macroscopic Dental Pathology of Some Earlier Human Populations. In: Dental Anthropology, edited by Don R. Brothwell. Symposia of the Society for the Study of Human Biology 5:271-88. New York: Pergamon Press.

1965 Digging Up Bones: The Excavation, Treatment and Study of Human Skeletal Remains. London: British Museum.

Brown, Antoinette B.

1973 Bone Strontium as a Dietary Indicator in Human Skeletal Populations. Ph.D. Dissertation, University of Michigan, University Microfilms, Ann Arbor, Michigan.

Brown, James A.

1971 The Dimensions of Status in the Burials at Spiro. In: Approaches to the Social Dimensions of Mortuary Practices, edited by James A. Brown. Society for American Archaeology Memoir 25:92-112.

Buikstra, Jane E.

1972 Hopewell in the Lower Illinois River Valley: A Regional Approach to the Study of Biological Variability and Mortuary Activity. Unpublished Ph.D. Dissertation, Department of Anthropology, University of Chicago.

1976 The Caribou Eskimo: General and Specific Disease. American Journal of Physical Anthropology 45:351-67.

1977a Biocultural Dimensions of Archaeological Study: A Regional Perspective. In: Biocultural Adaptation in Prehistoric America, edited by Robert L. Blakely. Southern Anthropological Society Proceedings 11:67-84.

1977b Differential Diagnosis: An Epidemiological Model. Yearbook of Physical Anthropology 1976, Yearbook Series 20:316-28.

Coale, Ansley J., and Paul Demeny

1966 Regional Model Life Tables and Stable Populations, Princeton: Princeton University Press.

Chapman, Carl, and Leo O. Anderson

1955 The Campbell Site: A Late Mississippi Town Site and Cemetery in Southeast Missouri. The Missouri Archaeologist 17(2 and 3).

Cook, Sherburne F., and Robert F. Heizer

1968 Relationships Among Houses, Settlement Areas, and Population in Aboriginal California. In: Settlement Archaeology, edited by Kwang-chih Chang, pp. 79-116. Palo Alto, California: National Press Books.

Corruccini, Robert S.
1974 An Examination of the Meaning of Cranial Discrete Traits for Human Skeletal Biological Studies. American Journal of Physical Anthropology 40:425-46.

Dahlberg, Albert A.
1951 The Dentition of the American Indian. In: The Physical Anthropology of the American Indian, edited W. S. Laughlin. The Viking Fund 5:138-76.
1963 Dental Traits as Identification Tools. Dental Progress 3:155-60.

DeJarnette, David, and Christopher S. Peebles
1970 The Development of Alabama Archaeology I: The Snow's Bend Site. Journal of Alabama Archaeology 16.

Dowd, John T.
1972 The West Site: A Stone Box Cemetery in Middle Tennessee. Tennessee Archaeological Society Miscellaneous Paper 10.

Dreizen, S. C., E. Currie, J. Gilley, and T. D. Spies
1956 Observations on the Association Between Nutritive Failure, Skeletal Maturation Rate and Radiopaque Lines in the Distal End of the Radius in Children. American Journal of Roentgenology 76:482-87.

Freeman, Murray F., and John W. Tukey
1950 Transformations Related to the Angular and the Square Root. Annals of Mathematical Statistics 21:607-11.

Funkhouser, William D., and William S. Webb
1931 The Duncan Site on the Kentucky-Tennessee Line. University of Kentucky Reports in Archaeology and Anthropology 1(6).

Génoves, Santiago
1967 Proportionality of the Long Bones and their Relation to Stature among Mesoamericans. American Journal of Physical Anthropology 26:67-77.

Giles, Eugene
1970 Discriminant Function Sexing of the Human Skeleton. In: Personal Identification in Mass Disasters, edited Thomas D. Stewart, pp. 99-109. Washington, D.C.: Smithsonian Institution.

Giles, Eugene, and Orville Elliot
1963 Sex Determination by Discriminant Function Analysis of Crania. American Journal of Physical Anthropology 21:53-68.

Gilmore, Melvin R.
1934 The Plight of Living Scalped Indians. Papers of the Michigan Academy of Science, Arts and Letters, 1933. 19:39-45.

Goldstein, Lynne G.
1976 Spatial Structure and Social Organization: Regional Manifestations of Mississippian Society. Unpublished Ph.D. Dissertation, Department of Anthropology, Northwestern University.

Goldstein, Marcus S.
1932 Congenital Absence and Impaction of the Third Molar in the Eskimo Mandible. American Journal of Physical Anthropology 16:381-88.
1948 Dentition of Indian Crania from Texas. American Journal of Physical Anthropology, n.s. 6:63-84.

Green, R. F., and J. M. Suchey
1976 The Use of Inverse Sine Transformation in the Analysis of Non-metrical Cranial Data. American Journal of Physical Anthropology 45:61-68.

Green, Sheryl, Stanton Green, and Georges J. Armelagos
1974 Settlement and Mortality of the Christian Site (1050 A.D.–1300 A.D.) of Meinarti (Sudan). Journal of Human Evolution 3:297-316.

Griffin, James B.
1967 Eastern North American Archaeology: A Summary. Science 156:175-91.

Hamperl, H.
1967 The Osteological Consequences of Scalping. In: Diseases in Antiquity, edited by Don R. Brothwell and A. T. Sandison, pp. 630-34, Springfield: C. C. Thomas.

Harn, Alan D.
1971 The Prehistory of Dickson Mounds: A Preliminary Report. Dickson Mounds Museum Anthropological Studies 1.

Hatch, James Willis
1974 Dallas Mortuary Practices. Unpublished M.A. Thesis, Pennsylvania State University.

Hatch, James Willis and Patrick S. Willey
1974 Stature and Status in Dallas Society. Tennessee Archaeologist 30:107-31.

Hooton, Earnest A.
1920 Indian Village Site and Cemetery Near Madisonville Ohio. Papers of the Peabody Museum of American Archaeology and Ethnology 8(1). Cambridge: Harvard University.
1946 Up From the Ape, rev. ed. New York: MacMillan.

Keen, J. A.
1950 A Study of the Differences Between Male and Female Skulls. American Journal of Physical Anthropology, n.s. 8:65-79.

Kerley, Ellis R.
1965 The Microscopic Determination of Age in Human Bone. American Journal of Physical Anthropology 23:149-63.
1969 Age Determination of Bone Fragments. Journal of Forensic Sciences 14:59-67.
1970 Estimation of Skeletal Age: After About Age 30. In: Personal Identification in Mass Disasters, edited by T. Dale Stewart, pp. 57-70. Washington, D.C.: Smithsonian Institution.

Klippel, Walter E.
1969 The Hearnes Site: A Multicomponent Occupation Site and Cemetery in the Cairo Lowland Region of Southeast Missouri. The Missouri Archaeologist 31.

Koritzer, Richard T.
1968 Apparent Tooth Preparation in a Middle Mississippi Indian Culture. Journal of Dental Research 47:839.

Kreshover, S. J.
1960 Metabolic Disturbances in Tooth Formation. Annals of the New York Academy of Science 85:161-67.

Lane, Rebecca A., and Audrey Sublett
1972 The Osteology of Social Organization: Residence Pattern. American Antiquity 37:186-201.

Marshall, Richard
1965 An Archaeological Investigation of Interstate 55 Through New Madrid and Pemiscot Counties, Missouri, 1964. Highway Archaeology Report No. 1, Missouri State Highway Department. Columbia: University of Missouri.

Marshall, W. A.
1968 Problems in Relating the Presence of Transverse Lines in the Radius to the Occurrence of Disease. In: The Skeletal Biology of Earlier Human Populations, edited by Don R. Brothwell, pp. 245-61. New York: Pergamon Press.

McHenry, Henry
1968 Transverse Lines in Long Bones of Prehistoric California Indians. American Journal of Physical Anthropology 29:1-18.

McKern, T. W., and Thomas D. Stewart
1957 Skeletal Age Changes in Young American Males, Analyzed from the Stand-

point of Identification. Technical Report EP-45. Natick, Mass: Headquarters Quartermaster Research and Development Command.

McWilliams, Kenneth R.
1974 Gran Quivira and Biological Distance in the U.S. Southwest. Ph.D. Dissertation, Arizona State University, University Microfilms, Ann Arbor, Michigan.

Miles, A. E. W.
1963 The Dentition in the Assessment of Individual Age. In: Dental Anthropology, edited by Don R. Brothwell. Symposia of the Society for the Study of Human Biology 5:191-209. New York: Pergamon Press.

Moore, J. A., Alan C. Swedlund, and G. J. Armelagos
1975 The Use of Life Tables in Paleodemography. In: Population Studies in Archaeology and Biological Anthropology: A Symposium, edited by Alan C. Swedlund. Society for American Archaeology Memoir 30:57-70.

Moorrees, C. F. A., E. A. Fanning, and E. E. Hunt, Jr.
1963 Age Variation of Formation Stages for Ten Permanent Teeth. Journal of Dental Research 42:1490-1502.

Morse, Dan F.
1969 Ancient Disease in the Midwest. Illinois State Museum Report of Investigations 15. Springfield, Illinois.

Naroll, Raoul
1962 Floor Area and Settlement Population. American Antiquity 27:587-89.

Nash, Charles H.
1962 Burials at the Lawhorn Site. The Missouri Archaeologist 24:99-103.

Newman, Marshall T., and Charles E. Snow
1942 Preliminary Report on the Skeletal Material from the Pickwick Basin, Alabama. In: An Archaeological Survey of Pickwick Basin in the Adjacent Portions of the States of Alabama, Mississippi, and Tennessee, by William S. Webb and David L. DeJarnette. Smithsonian Institution Bureau of American Ethnology Bulletin 129.

Owsley, Douglas W., and Hugh E. Berryman
1975 Ethnographic and Archaeological Evidence of Scalping in the Southeastern United States. Tennessee Archaeologist 31:41-58.

Pearson, Karl
1899 On the Reconstruction of the Stature of Prehistoric Races. Philosophical Transactions of the Royal Society, London, Series A (Mathematical) 192: 169-244.

Peebles, Christopher S.
1971 Moundville and Surrounding Sites: Some Structural Considerations of Mortuary Practices II. In: Approaches to the Social Dimensions of Mortuary Practices, edited by James A. Brown. Society for American Archaeology Memoir 25:68-91.
1974 Moundville: The Organization of a Prehistoric Community and Culture. Unpublished Ph.D. Dissertation, Department of Anthropology, University of California, Santa Barbara.

Perino, Gregory
1966 The Banks Village Site, Crittenden County, Arkansas. Missouri Archaeological Society Memoir 4.

Perzigian, Anthony J.
1975 Natural Selection on the Dentition of an Arikara Population. American Journal of Physical Anthropology 42:63-70.

Phenice, Terrell W.
1969a A Newly Developed Visual Method of Sexing the Os Pubis. American Journal of Physical Anthropology 30:297-302.

1969b An Analysis of the Human Skeletal Material from Burial Mounds in North Central Kansas. University of Kansas Publications in Anthropology 1.

Price, James E.

1973 Settlement Planning and Artifact Distribution on the Snodgrass Site and Their Socio-Political Implications in the Powers Phase of Southeast Missouri. Ph.D. Dissertation, University of Michigan, University Microfilms, Ann Arbor, Michigan.

Price, James E. and James B. Griffin

1979 The Snodgrass Site of the Powers Phase of Southeast Missouri. Museum of Anthropology, University of Michigan, Anthropological Papers 66.

Redfield, Alden

1970 A New Aid to Aging Immature Skeletons: Development of the Occipital Bone. American Journal of Physical Anthropology 33:207-20.

Rightmire, George Phillip

1972 Cranial Measurements and Discrete Traits Compared in Distance Studies of African Negro Skulls. Human Biology 44:263-76.

Robbins, Louise M.

1971 The High Incidence of Bone Pathologies in Fort Ancient Peoples of Kentucky. Paper presented at the meetings of the American Association of Physical Anthropologists. Boston.

Romero, Javier

1958 Mutilaciones dentarias prehispánicas de México y América en general. Instituto Nacional de Antropologiá e Historia, Serie Investigaciónes 3. Mexico.

Saxe, Arthur A.

1970 Social Dimensions of Mortuary Practices. Ph.D. Dissertation, University of Michigan, University Microfilms, Ann Arbor, Michigan.

1971 Social Dimensions of Mortuary Practices in a Mesolithic Population from Wadi Halfa, Sudan. In: Approaches to the Social Dimensions of Mortuary Practices, edited by James A. Brown. Society for American Archaeology Memoir 25:39-57.

Schuman, E. L., and C. Loring Brace

1955 Metric and Morphological Variations in the Definition of the Liberian Chimpanzee: Comparisons with Anthropoid and Human Dentitions. In: The Non-Human Primates and Human Evolution, edited by James E. Gavan, pp. 61-90. Detroit: Wayne State University Press.

Sears, William

1968 The State and Settlement Patterns in the New World. In: Settlement Archaeology, edited by Kwang-chih Chang, pp. 134-45. Palo Alto, California: National Press Books.

Singer, R.

1953 Estimation of Age from Cranial Suture Closure: A Report on Its Unreliability. Journal of Forensic Medicine 1:52-59.

Singh, I. J., and D. L. Gunberg

1970 Estimation of Age at Death in Human Bones from quantitative Histology of Bone Fragments. American Journal of Physical Anthropology 33:373-82.

Sjovold, Torstein

1973 The Occurrence of Minor Non-metrical Variants in the Skeleton and their Quantitative Treatment for Population Comparisons. Homo 24:204-33.

Snow, Charles E.

1941a Anthropological Studies at Moundville, Part 1: Indian Skeletons from the Museum Burials at Moundville. Alabama Museum of Natural History Anthropological Studies, Museum Paper 15.

1941b Anthropological Studies at Moundville, Part 2: Possible Evidence of Scalping at Moundville. Alabama Museum of Natural History Anthropological Studies, Museum Paper 15.

Sokal, Robert R., and F. James Rohlf

1969 Biometry. San Francisco: W. H. Freeman.

Spence, Michael W.

1974 Residential Practices and the Distribution of Skeletal Traits in Teotihuacan, Mexico. Man 9:262-73.

Spier, Robert F. G.

1955 Skeletal Remains from the Campbell Site. In: The Campbell Site: A Late Mississippi Site and Cemetery in Southeast Missouri by Carl Haley Chapman and L. O. Anderson. The Missouri Archaeologist 17 (2 and 3).

Steele, D. Gentry, and Thomas W. McKern

1969 A Method for Assessment of Maximum Long Bone Length and Living Stature from Fragmentary Long Bones. American Journal of Physical Anthropology 31:215-28.

Stewart, Thomas Dale

1943 Skeletal Remains from Platte and Clay Counties, Missouri. In: Archaeological Investigations in Platte and Clay Counties Missouri by Waldo R. Wedel. Smithsonian Institution U.S. National Museum Bulletin 183:245-74.

1948 Medico-legal Aspects of the Skeleton. I. Age, Sex, Race, and Stature. American Journal of Physical Anthropology 31:417-26.

Stini, William A.

1969 Nutritional Stress and Growth: Sex Differences in Adaptive Response. American Journal of Physical Anthropology 31:417-26.

Swanton, John R.

1911 Indian Tribes of the Lower Mississippi Valley and Adjacent Coast of the Gulf of Mexico. Smithsonian Institution Bureau of American Ethnology Bulletin 43.

Tainter, Joseph Anthony

1975 The Archaeological Study of Social Change: Woodland Systems in West-Central Illinois. Ph.D. Dissertation, Northwestern University. University Microfilms, Ann Arbor.

Trotter, Mildred, and Goldine C. Gleser

1952 Estimation of Stature from Long Bones of American Whites and Negroes. American Journal of Physical Anthropology 10:463-514.

1958 A Re-evaluation of Estimation of Stature Based on Measurements of Stature Taken During Life and of Long Bones After Death. American Journal of Physical Anthropology 16:79-123.

Ubelaker, Douglas H.

1974 Reconstruction of Demographic Profiles from Ossuary Skeletal Remains: A Case Study from the Tidewater Potomac. Smithsonian Contributions to Anthropology 18.

1978 Human Skeletal Remains: Excavation, Analysis, Interpretation. Chicago: Aldine Publishing.

Ubelaker, Douglas H., T. W. Phenice, and W. M. Bass

1969 Artificial Interproximal Grooving of the Teeth in American Indians. American Journal of Physical Anthropology 30:145-49.

Vogel, J. C., and Nikolaas J. Van der Merwe

1976 Isotopic Evidence for Early Maize Cultivation in New York State. Paper presented at the meetings of the Society for American Archaeology, St. Louis.

Wallace, John A.
1974 Approximal Grooving of Teeth. American Journal of Physical Anthropology 40:385-90.

Washburn, S. L.
1948 Sex Differences in the Pubic Bone. American Journal of Physical Anthropology n.s. 6:199-208.

Weiss, Kenneth M.
1973 Demographic Models for Anthropology. Society for American Archaeology Memoir 27.

White, Patsy
1970 Investigation of the Cemetery at the Gee's Landing Site, 3DR17. The Arkansas Archeologist 11:1-20.

Wissler, Clark
1920 North American Indians of the Plains. New York: American Museum of Natural History.

Wright, Moira H. M., D. C. Stone, and W. M. Bass
1973 Skeletal Material from the West Site, 40DV12, Davidson County, Tennessee. Tennessee Archaeologist 29:12-50.

Plate 1. Turner site, Burial 5, facing east. Individual B is on top, C is on the left, and A is on the right. Note the generally poor preservation of the bone, as shown by the lack of ribs, vertebrae, hands, feet, and long bone epiphyses.

Plate 2. Turner site, Burial 13, facing north. The extended individuals are from north to south, A, B, and C. Individuals D and E are in a bundle lying on the femora of C. Again, note the poor preservation.

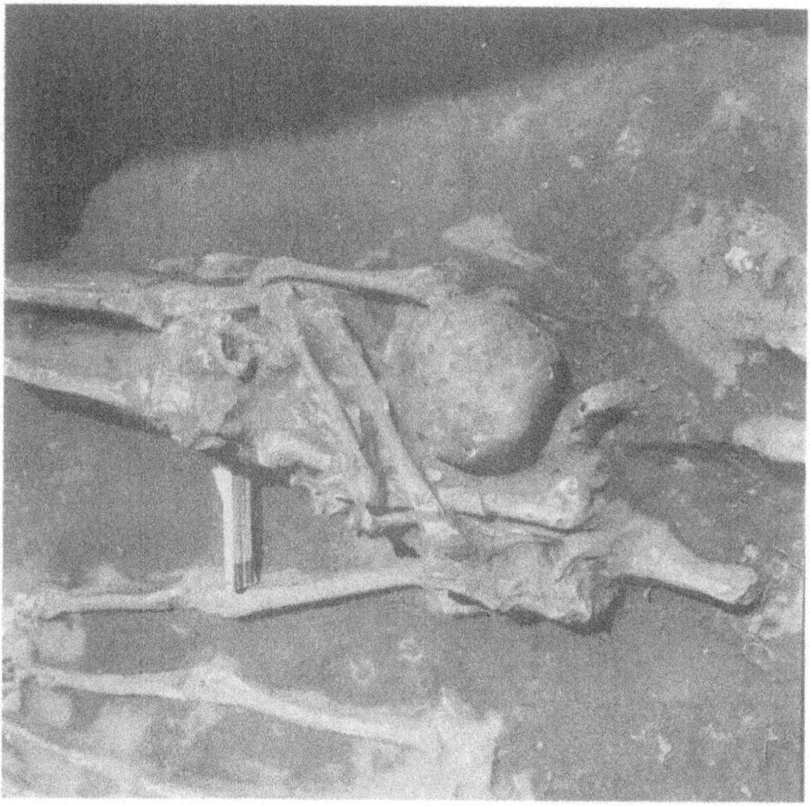

Plate 3. Turner site, Burial 13, facing east. This is a close-up of Individuals D and E. The numerous holes in the bones do not represent multiple myeloma; they were made by a pothunter's probe.

Plate 4. Turner site, Burial 15, facing east. This is the only burial accompanied by a dog. It is also unusual because the legs of B-15 are not both extended.

Plate 5. Turner site, Burial 18, facing south. B-18 was a badly disturbed, poorly preserved, multiple burial.

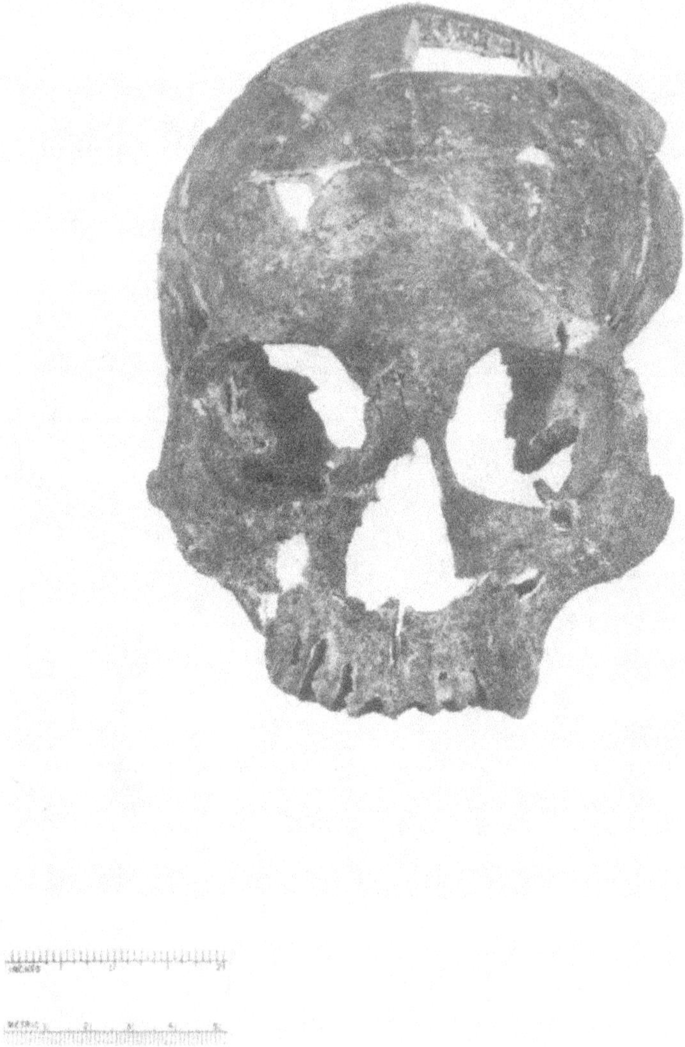

Plate 6. Turner site, "Burial 61," Individual A, facial view. This is one of the few faces which could be reconstructed. Although it is incomplete, the face of this woman appears to be fairly characteristic of the Powers phase population, at least on the basis of comparison to the fragmentary faces of some other skeletons.

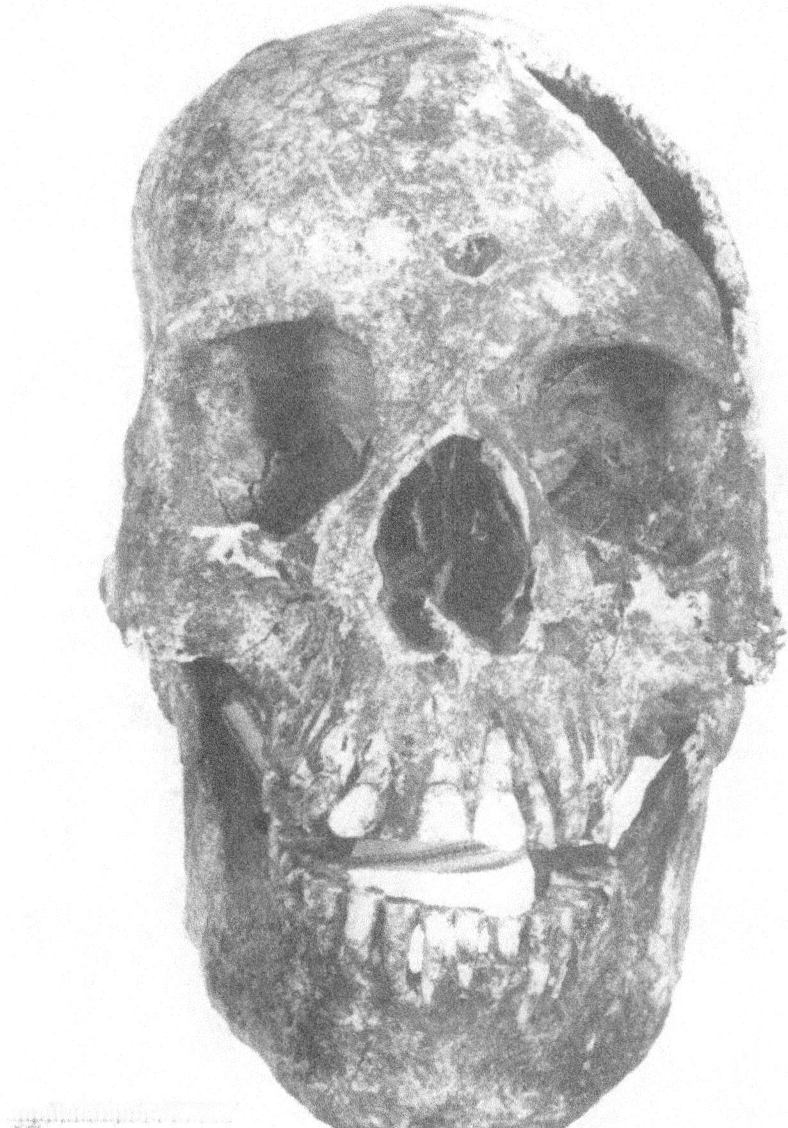

Plate 7A. Turner site, Burial 13, Individual C, facial view. This female is rather uncharacteristic of the Powers phase population. Her head is relatively longer, higher, and narrower than was typical.

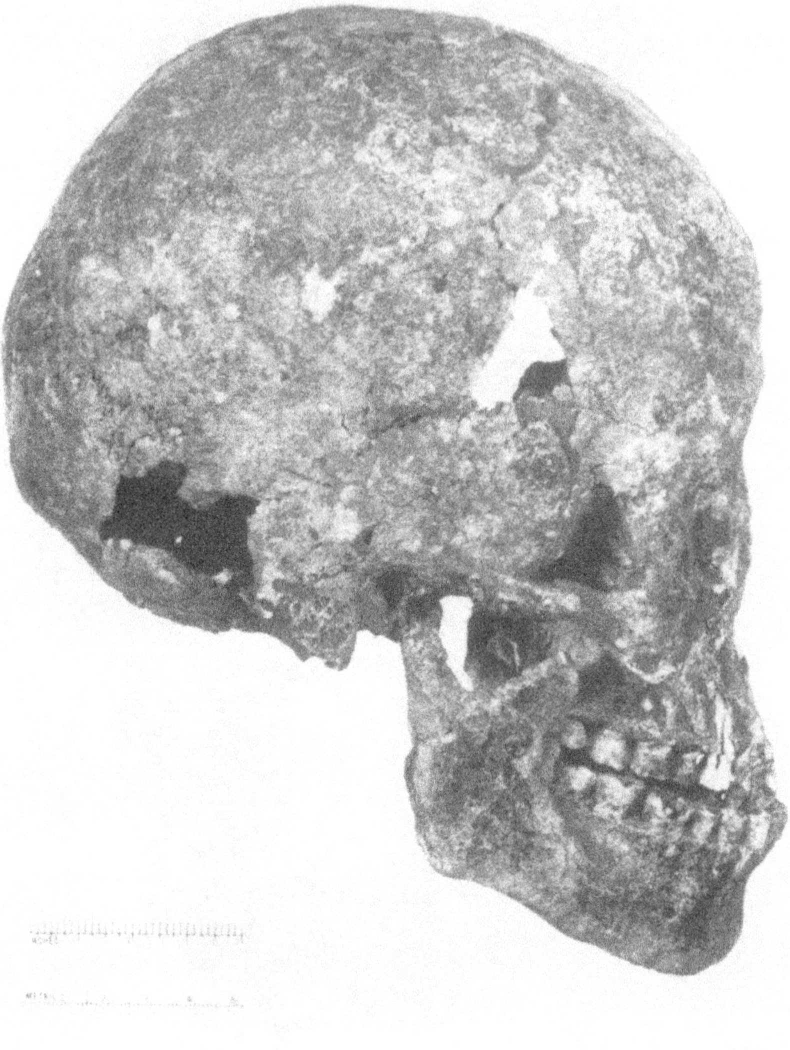

Plate 7B. Turner site, Burial 13, Individual C, lateral view.

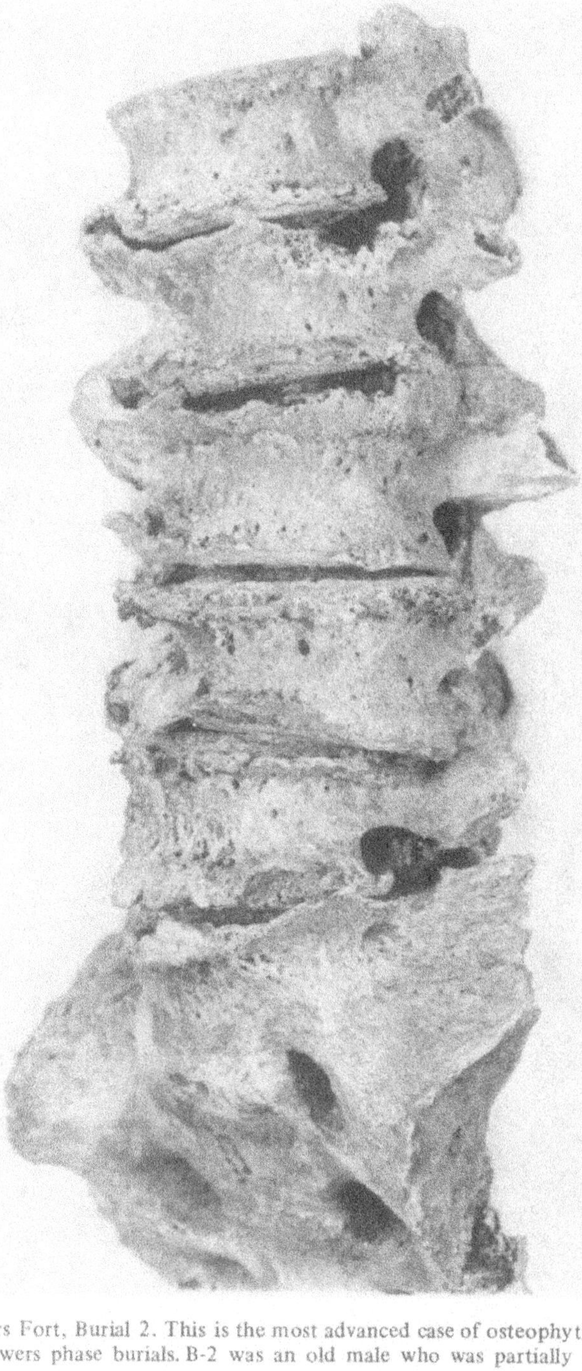

Plate 8. Powers Fort, Burial 2. This is the most advanced case of osteophytic lipping of any of the Powers phase burials. B-2 was an old male who was partially crippled by arthritis.

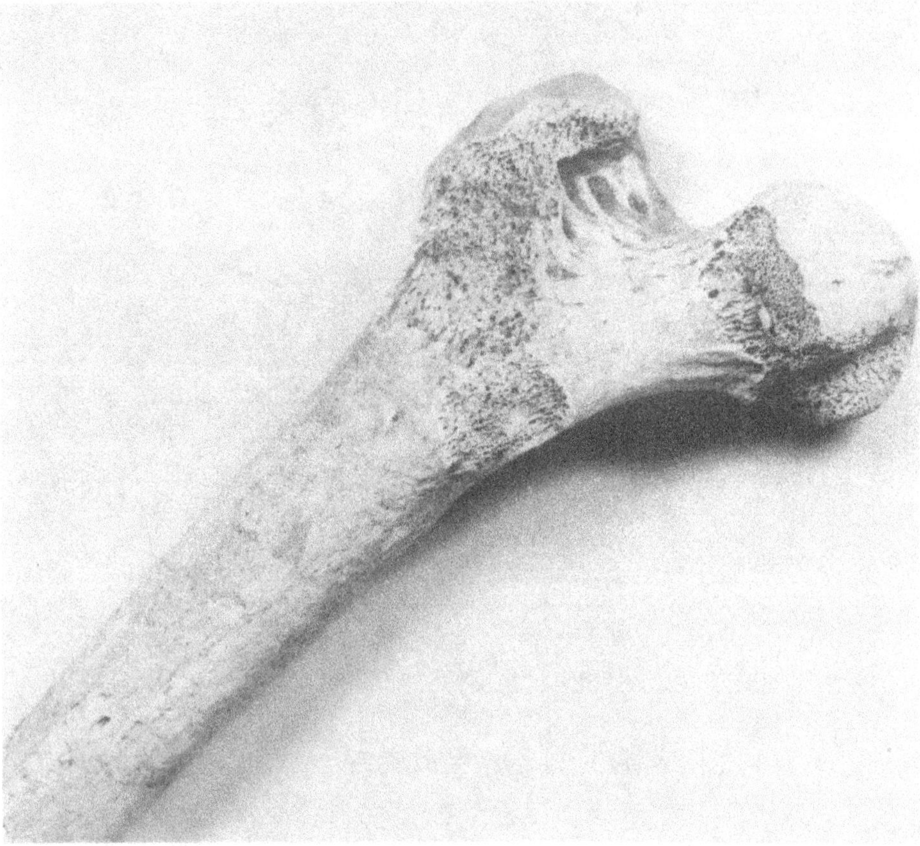

Plate 9. Powers Fort, Burial 1. The tip of a chert projectile point is visible in the exposed cancellous bone at the junction of the femoral head and neck on the posterior side of the left femur. This 30-year-old male appears to have been shot from behind.

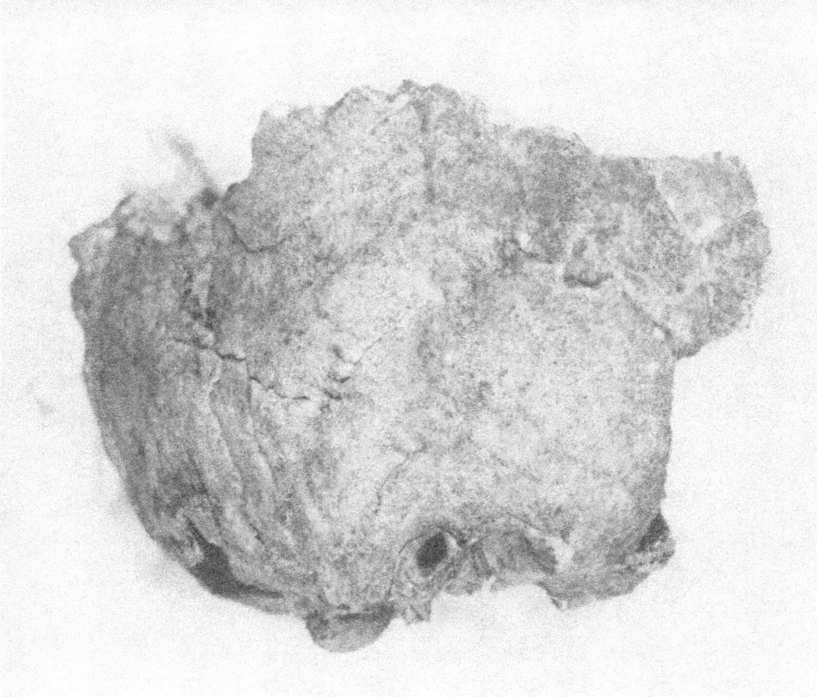

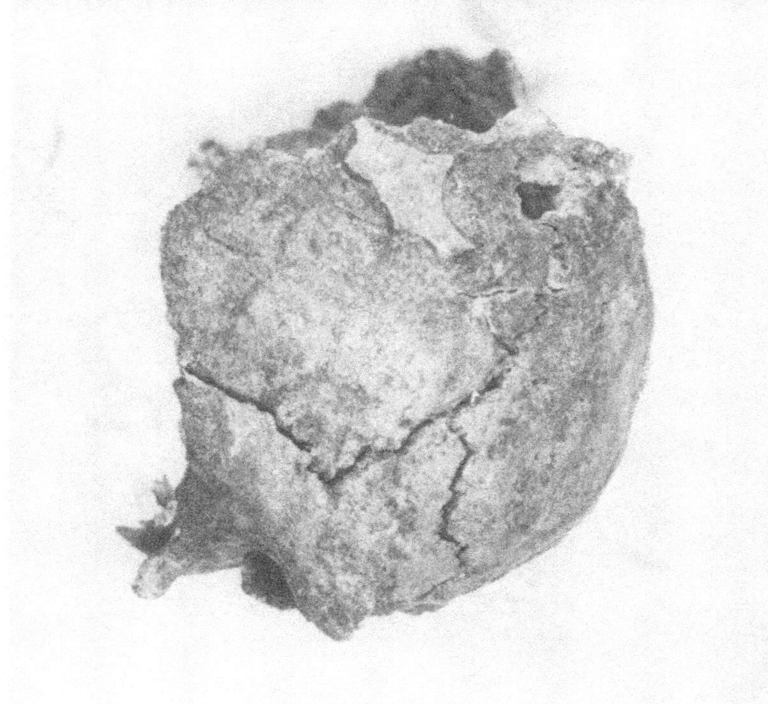

Plates 10A and 10B. Powers Fort, Burial 6, left and right lateral views. The outer table of the cranium of this female has been eroded, apparently as the result of an infection. The erosion took the form of a circle girdling the skull, leaving isolated islands of unaffected bone (Pl. 10A) and completely eroding the cranial bone in other areas (from lambda to right asterion). Poor preservation and the thinning of the bone prevented the reconstruction of the skull.

Appendixes

Appendix A

TABLE 59 Individuals Aged by the Development of the Occipital*

Site	*Individual*	*Age*
23BU21A	Burial 41A	about 8-12 yr.
23BU21A	Structure 27 B-1	less than 3 mo.
23BU21B	Structure 42 B-1	less than 3 mo.
23BU21B	Structure 42 B-2	less than 3 mo.
23BU21B	Structure 44 B-1	less than 3 mo.
23BU21B	Structure 47 B-1	less than 3 mo.
23BU21B	Structure 50 B-1	less than 3 mo.
23BU21B	Structure 77 B-1	less than 3 mo.
23BU10	Structure 1 B-1	less than 3 mo.
23BU10	Structure 1 B-2	3-6 mo.
23BU10	Structure 1 B-3	less than 3 mo.

*Standards from Redfield (1970)

TABLE 60 Individuals Aged by Dental Calcification and Eruption*

Site	*Individual*	*Calcification*	*Eruption*
23BU21A	B-3	5.5±1	
23BU21A	B-6C		less than 11
23BU21A	B-8C	6.0±2	
23BU21A	B-13A	15.1±2	
23BU21A	B-13D	16.1±2.5	
23BU21A	B-19A	9.5±1.5	
23BU21A	B-22C	4.9±1	
23BU21A	B-25B	6.3±1	
23BU21A	B-28A	15.5±2	
23BU21A	B-29	5.0±1	
23BU21A	B-31B	6.1±1	
23BU21A	B-33C	5.8±1	
23BU21A	B-37A	1.8±0.5	
23BU21A	B-38A or D	5.5±1.5	
23BU21A	B-38E	15.8±2	
23BU21A	B-52A	11.4±2.5	
23BU21A	B-55B	5.4±1	
23BU21A	B-56		2.5±1
23BU21A	B-57	1.9±0.5	
23BU21A	B-59	7.5±1	
23BU21B	B-4B		2.0±1

*Standards from Moorrees, Fanning and Hunt (1963) and Brothwell (1965)

TABLE 61 Individuals Aged by Dental Attrition

Burial	*Age*	*Estimate of Error*	*Burial*	*Age*	*Estimate of Error*
23BU21A			23BU21A		
6A	37	±8	36A	28	±5
7	32	±5	36B	21	±2
8A	42	±8	47	34	±8
8B	30	±5	49	59	±10
8D	40	±8	51	38	±8
11A	51	±10	52B	22	±3
11B	21	±2	52C	55	±10
13B	46	±10	52D	35	±8
13C	37	±8	53A	29	±5
15	41	±8	53B	52	±10
16A	26	±5	54A	22	±3
18C	57	±10	55C	32	±8
18D	25	±4	55D	34	±8
20	44	±10	61A	20	±2
22A	42	±8	61B	32	±5
23	25	±4	61C	20	±2
24B	31	±5	61D	48	±10
24C	36	±8	61E	65	±10
24D	39	±8	23BU21B		
25A	43	±8	3	20	±2
27	54	±10	4A	43	±8
30	50	±10	7	22	±3
33A	23	±3	23BU10		
34	27	±5	1	30	±5
35A	20	±2	2	68	±10
35B	38	±8	3	62	±10
35C	33	±5			

Appendix B

TABLE 62 Pelvic Sex

Burial	*Sex*	*Burial*	*Sex*
23BU21A		23BU21A	
1	I*	35A	F?#
5 P-1	F	35B	F
5 P-2	F	36A	M?
6 or 11	I	36B	F
7	I	44	I
8?	I	47	I
12A	I	48	F
13A	F?	49	F
13B	F	52 P-1	I
15	F	52 P-2	I
18A	I	53 P-1	F
20	I	53 P-2	I
21A	M	55 P-1	M
21B	I	55 P-2	F
22?	I	61 P-1	F
23	M	61 P-2	F
24 P-1	M	61 P-3	I
24 P-2	I	61 P-4	I
24 P-3	I	61 P-5	I
25A	F?	23BU21B	
26	I	1	I
27	F	3	F
28?	I	4A	I
31A	I	7	F
31C	M	23BU10	
33A	M	1	M
33B	M?	2	M
34	F		

*I = indeterminate sex
#Narrow sciatic notch, but very deep sulcus

TABLE 63 Cranial Sex

Burial	*Sex*	*Burial*	*Sex*
23BU21A		23BU21A	
2 CF-1	M	38?	I
6A	I*	40	I
7	F	47	I
8A	I	49	I
8D	M	51	M
12A	I	52 CF-1	M
13A	F	53A	F
13B	F	53B	F
13C	F	54 CF-1	M
15	F	55C	M
16A	M	55D	M
18C	I(M?)	58	M
20	M	60	M
21A	M	61A	F
22A	M	61 CF-2	F
23	I	61 CF-3	F
24A	M	loose skull	M
25A	F?	23BU21B	
27	I(M?)	3	F
28A	I	4	M
33A	M	7	F
33B	M	23BU10	
34	F	1	M
35A	F	2	M
35B	F	3A	M
36A	M	3B	M
36B	F	6	F
38E	F		

*I = indeterminate sex

TABLE 64 Sex from Femur Circumference at Midshaft

Individual	*Side*	*Circumference*	*Femoral Sex*	*Comments*
23BU21B				
1 F-1	L	79.5	F	
3	A*	80.2	F	
7	A	71.2	F	
STR 19 burned	R	73.0	F	may not be Powers phase
23BU10				
1	A	91.2	M	
2	A	93.8	M	
3A	L	106.0	M	measured below midshaft
6	A	68.0	F	
23BU21A				
2 F-1	R	75.0	F	measured above midshaft
2 F-2	L	90.0	M	
5A	A	89.8	M	
5B	L	73.0	F	
6 F-3	R	86.0	M	
6 F-11	R	81.5	F	
6&11 F-4&5	A	80.0	F	
6&11 F-1&8	A	80.7	F	
6&11 F-2&9	A	76.8	F	
6&11 F-7	R	84.5	I#	
11 F-6&10	A	81.0	F	
7	R	75.0	F	
8 F-2&4	A	92.5	M	
8 F-1&5	L	91.5	M	
8 F-3,6&7	A	80.5	F	
12A	A	80.0	F	
12B	A	74.0	F	
13A	A	71.8	F	
13B	A	80.7	F	
13D or E	A	87.0	M	
15	L	79.5	F	
16 F-1	R	70.0	F	
18A	A	78.5	F	
18B	R	73.0	F	
18C	?	75.5	F	
18D	R	81.0	F	
19B	A	78.8	F	
20	A	88.5	M	
21B	?	75.0	F	
22?	A	97.0	M	
23	A	88.5	M	
24A	A	88.7	M	
24C or D	A	74.5	F	
24C or D	L	78.5	F	
25A	A	76.5	F	

TABLE 64, cont.

Individual		*Side*	*Circumference*	*Femoral Sex*	*Comments*
23BU21A (cont.)					
26	F-1&2	A	88.0	M	
26	F-3	R?	94.5	M	extra femur, may not belong in burial
27		R	82.0	F	
28	F-2&3	A	65.5	F	
28	F-4&6	A	75.2	F	
28	F-1	R	69.5	F	
28	F-5	R	86.5	M	may not belong to this burial
30		?	76.5	F	
31A		R	79.5	F	
32		L	75.5	F	
33A		A	97.2	M	
33B		A	92.8	M	
34		L	76.0	F	
35A		R	80.5	F	
35B		A	75.5	F	
35C		R	79.5	F	
36A		A	92.2	M	
36B		A	68.0	F	
37B		?	70.0	F	
38B		R	80.5	F	
38E		?	61.5	F	
38?		L	89.5	M	measured above midshaft
40		A	79.2	F	
41B		A	66.7	F	
45		A	76.2	F	
46		L	91.5	M	measured above midshaft
47		A	83.0	F	
48		A	70.5	F	
49	F-1	R	74.0	F	
49	F-2	L	85.5	I	may not belong to this burial
52	F-2&7	A	77.2	F	these are the extended femora
52	F-1&6	A	91.0	M	
52	F-3	L	78.5	F	
52	F-4&5	R	90.7	M	measured above midshaft
53	F-1&3	A	73.5	F	
53	F-2&4	A	77.5	F	
55	F-3	L	75.0	F	
55	F-4	R	95.5	M	measured below midshaft
58	F-1	R	83.5	F	measured above midshaft
60		A	96.8	M	
61	F-1&10	A	81.0	F	
61	F-5&8	A	83.0	F	
61	F-2&11	A	85.8	M	
61	F-6&9	A	76.2	F	

TABLE 64, cont.

Individual	*Side*	*Circumference*	*Femoral Sex*	*Comments*
23BU21A (cont.)				
61 F-4&7	A	73.5	F	
61 F-12	R	79.0	F	measured above midshaft
61 F-3	R	90.0	M	measured well below midshaft
STR 32 FS 62	L	62.5	F	may belong to a burial

*The average of left and right
#Indeterminate sex

Appendix C

TABLE 65 Minimum Count of Individuals per Burial on the Bases of Age and Sex

Burial	*Cranial*	*Pelvic*	*Femoral*	*Other*	*Total*	
23BU21B						
1	2I	1I	1F,1I		1F,1I	
3	1F	1F	1F		1F	
4	1M,1J	1I			1M,1J	
7	1F	1F	1F		1F	
STR 19	1I		1F		1F	
23BU10						
1	1M	1M	1M		1M	
2	1M	1M	1M		1M	
3	2M		1M		2M	
6	1F		1F		1F	
23BU21A						
1		1I			1I	(2)
2	1M		1M,1F		1M,1F	
3	1J				1J	
4				lower legs	1I	
5		2F,1J	1M,1F,1J		1M,2F,1J	
6,11,(42)	4I,1J	1I	1M,5F,1I		1M,5F,1I,1J	
7	1F	1I	1F		1F	
8(9)	1M,2I,1J	1I	2M,1F		2M,1F,1J	
10				small fragments	1I	
12	1I	1I	2F		2F	
13	3F,1I	2F	1M,2F		1M,3F	(1)
14	1J				1J	
15	1F	1F	1F		1F	
16	1M		1F		1M,1F	
18	2I	1F,1I	4F		4F	
19	1J		1F		1F,1J	
20	1M	1I	1M		1M	
21	1M	1M,1I	1F,1I		1M,1F	
22	1M,1I,1J	1I	1M		1M,1I,1J	
23	1I	1M	1M		1M	

TABLE 65, cont.

Burial	*Cranial*	*Pelvic*	*Femoral*	*Other*	*Total*	
<u>23BU21A</u> (cont.)						
24	1M,3I	1M,2I	1M,2F		1M,2F,1I	
25	1F,1J	1F	1F		1F,1J	
26	1I	1I	1M,1M*		1M,1M*	
27	1I	1F	1F		1F	
28	3I	1I	3F,1M*		3F,1M*	
29	1J			vert. of J	1J	
30	1I		1F		1F	
31(50)	1J	1M,1I	1F,1J		1M,1F,1J	
32			1F		1F	
33	2M,1J	2M	2M		2M,1J	
34	1F	1F	1F		1F	
35	2F,1I,1J	2F	3F		3F,1J	
36	1M,1F	1M,1F	1M,1F,1I*		1M,1F,1I*	
37	1J		1F		1F,1J	
38(17)	1F,1I,1J		1M,2F,2J		1M,2F,2J	
39				remains not located		(1J)
40	1I		1F		1F	
41	1I,1J		1F		1F,1J	
43						(1I)
44	1I	1I			1I	
45	1I		1F		1F	
46			1M		1M	
47	1I	1I	1F		1F	
48	1I	1F	1F		1F	
49	1I	1F	1F,1I*		1F,1I*	
51	1M			arm fragments	1M	
52	1M,2I,1J	2I	2M,2F,1J		2M,2F,1J	
53	2F	1F,1I	2F		2F	
54	1M*,2I*		1I*		1M*,2I*	
55	2M,2J	1M,1F	1M,1F		2M,1F,2J	
56	1J				1J	
57	1J				1J	
58	1M*		1F*		1M*,1F*	
59	1J		1J		1J	
60	1M	1I	1M		1M	
61(MHBB)	3F,2I	2F,3I	2M,5F		2M,5F	
STR32 FS62			1F*		1F*	
Stray Frag.	1M*				1M*	
<u>Totals</u>						
23BU21B	1M,2F, 3I,1J	2F,2I	4F,1I		1M,4F, 1I,1J	
23BU10	4M,1F	2M	3M,1F		4M,1F	

TABLE 65, cont.

Burial	*Cranial*	*Pelvic*	*Femoral*	*Other*	*Total*
23BU21A	18M,16F, 34I,20J (Includes the male crania from B-54,B-58, and "stray fragments", since these were complete enough that they are probably unrepresented elsewhere. The 2I* from B-54 are omitted.)	8M,18F, 23I,1J	22M,55F,2I,6J (omits femora with an * from burials 26,28,36,49,54,58, and STR 32, since they may belong to individuals already counted in other burials.)		27M,57F,7I, 22J (1 adult, 1 juvenile and 3 individuals of unknown age were found in the field but not in the lab.)

Key

J = juvenile (1-15); all others adult. Infants not included.

M = male, F = female, I = indeterminate sex.

When an * occurs next to any letter (F, M, I, or J), that individual may not belong in the burial. Consult Chapter 2 for details.

Numbers occurring in parentheses in the "Total" column represent additional individuals which were definitely observed in the burials by the excavators, but which were not located in the lab.

Appendix D

MINIMUM PARTS INVENTORY FOR POWERS PHASE BURIALS

Key

The column headings are names or simple abbreviations for bones or bony parts. "Ear" refers to the petrous part of the temporal. "IOP" is the internal occipital protuberance of the occipital bone. When the terms "Hand" and "Foot" are used, it means that at least one of the many bones of the hand or foot is present.

The column headings "L" and "R" refer to left and right, respectively. The column heading "U" means the side the bone came from is uncertain.

Under "Vert", the headings "C", "T", and "L" refer to cervical, thoracic, and lumbar vertebrae, respectively.

In the listings, an ordinary number represents an adult bone, an "I" represents an infant bone, and a "J" represents a juvenile bone (ages 1 to 15). A "P" is used when a bone is recognized to be present, but is in too many pieces to allow calculation of the minimum count.

TABLE 66 Powers Fort (23BU10) Minimum Parts Skeletal Inventory

	Burial								*Totals*		
	1	*2*	*3A*	*3B*	*6*	*STR 1 B-1*	*STR 1 B-2*	*STR 1 B-3*	*Adult*	*Infant*	*"Present"*
Max	1	1	1			I	I	I	3	3	
Mand	1	1	1	1		I	I	I	4	3	
Ear											
L	1	1	1	1	1	I	I	I	5	3	
R	1	1	1	1	1	I	I	I	5	3	
IOP	1	1	1	1	1		I		5	1	
Humerus											
L	1	1					I	I	2	2	
R	1	1				I	I	I	2	3	
U									0	0	
Radius											
L	1	1					I		2	1	
R	1	1					I	I	2	2	
U									0	0	
Ulna											
L	1	1					I		2	1	
R	1	1				I	I		2	2	
U									0	0	
Hand											
L		1							1	0	
R		1							1	0	
U									0	0	
Scap											
L	1	1							2	0	
R	1	1				I	I	I	2	3	
Clav											
L	1	1				I		I	2	2	
R		1					I	I	1	2	
Ster		1							1	0	
Ribs	P	P					I		0	1	2
Vert											
C		P				I	I		0	2	1
T	P	P				I	I	I	0	3	2
L	P	P							0	0	2
Sac	1	1							2	0	
Innom											
L	1	1					I	I	2	2	
R	1	1				I	I	I	2	3	
U									0	0	
Femur											
L	1	1	1		1		I	I	4	2	
R	1	1			1		I	I	3	2	
U									0	0	
Pat											
L									0	0	
R		1							1	0	

TABLE 66, cont.

	Burial								*Totals*		
	1	*2*	*3A*	*3B*	*6*	*STR 1 B-1*	*STR 1 B-2*	*STR 1 B-3*	*Adult*	*Infant*	*"Present"*
Tibia											
L	1	1			1		I	I	3	2	
R	1	1					I	I	2	2	
U									0	0	
Fibula											
L		1					I		1	1	
R		1					I		1	1	
U								I	0	1	
Foot											
L									0	0	
R		1						I	1	1	
U									0	0	

TABLE 67 Snodgrass Site (23BU21B) Minimum Parts Skeletal Inventory

Burial	Max	Mand	Ear		IOP	Humerus			Radius			Ulna			Hand			Scap		Clav		Ster
			L	*R*		*L*	*R*	*U*	*L*	*R*	*U*	*L*	*R*	*U*	*L*	*R*	*U*	*L*	*R*	*L*	*R*	
1		1	1	2	1																	
3	1	1	1	1	1	1	1		1	1		1	1					1	1	1		
4A	1	1	1	1	1					1			1							1		
4B	J	J	J	J	J																	
7	1	1	1	1	1	1	1											1	1	1	1	
STR 19 burned					1																	
STR 42 B-1			I	I																		
STR 42 B-2			I	I																		
STR 44 B-1		I	I	I		I	I												I			
STR 45 B-1														1				1				
STR 47 B-1		I	I	I																		
STR 48 B-1			I	I					I			I			I							
STR 50 B-1		I	I	I																		
STR 77 B-1			I	I	I																	
Adult totals	3	4	4	5	5	2	2	0	1	2	0	1	2	1	0	0	0	3	2	3	1	0
Juvenile totals	1	1	1	1	1	0	0	0	0	0	0	0	0	0	0	0	0	0	0	0	0	0
Infant totals	0	3	7	7	1	1	1	0	1	0	0	1	0	0	1	0	0	0	1	0	0	0

TABLE 67, cont.

Burial	Ribs	Vert			Sac	Inom			Femur			Pat		Tibia			Fibula			Foot		
		C	*T*	*L*		*L*	*R*	*U*	*L*	*R*	*U*	*L*	*R*	*L*	*R*	*U*	*L*	*R*	*U*	*L*	*R*	*U*
1								1	2	1				2	2		1	1				1
3	P	P	P	P	1	1	1		1	1		1	1	1	1		1	1		1	1	
4A		P	P			1				1		1	1	1	1		1	1		1	1	
4B																						
7	P	P	P						1	1				1	1							
STR 19 burned									1	1					1							
STR 42 B-1																						
STR 42 B-2	I		I																			
STR 44 B-1	I	I	I						I	I				I	I							
STR 45 B-1	P		P									1										
STR 47 B-1	I					I	I		I	I												
STR 48 B-1		I								I												
STR 50 B-1																						
STR 77 B-1																						
Adult totals					1	2	1	1	5	5	0	3	2	5	5	0	3	3	0	2	2	1
Juvenile totals	0	0	0	0	0	0	0	0	0	0	0	0	0	0	0	0	0	0	0	0	0	0
Infant totals	3	2	2	0	0	1	1	0	2	3	0	0	0	1	1	0	0	0	0	0	0	0
"Present" totals	3	3	4	1																		

TABLE 68 Turner Site (23BU21A) Minimum Parts Skeletal Inventory

			Ear			Humerus			Radius			Ulna			Hand			Scap		Clav		
Burial	*Max*	*Mand*	*L*	*R*	*IOP*	*L*	*R*	*U*	*L*	*R*	*U*	*L*	*R*	*U*	*L*	*R*	*U*	*L*	*R*	*L*	*R*	*Ster*
1											1			1								
2					1					1												
3	J	J	J	J	J																	
4																						
5A																			1			
5B										1			1									
5 (mixed)																						
6A	1	1	1		1																	
6B		1	1																			
6C	J		J	J																		
11A		1																				
11B	1	1																				
6 (long bones)								1,J														
11 (long bones)																						
6 & 11 (mixed)							1				2											
7	1	1	1	1	1		1													1	1	
8A	1	1	1	1	1																	
8B		1			1																	
8C	J	J																				
8D	1	1	1	1																		
8 (postcranial)						3	2			1			1							1		
10																	1			1		
12A	1	1	1		1		1															
12B																						

TABLE 68, cont.

		Vert				*Inom*			*Femur*			*Pat*		*Tibia*			*Fibula*			*Foot*		
Burial	*Ribs*	*C*	*T*	*L*	*Sac*	*L*	*R*	*U*	*L*	*R*	*U*	*L*	*R*	*L*	*R*	*U*	*L*	*R*	*U*	*L*	*R*	*U*
1	P						1	1														
2									1	1												
3																						
4														1	1		1	1		1	1	
5A	P		P						1	1		1	1	1	1		1	1		1	1	
5B									1		1			1	1				1	1	1	
5 (mixed)				P	1	2	2	J	J		J											
6A																						
6B																						
6C																						
11A																						
11B																						
6 (long bones)										2		1	1	1	1							
11 (long bones)									1	1												
6 & 11 (mixed)								1	1	5	3			2	3				P			
7						1			1	1			1	1	1				1			
8A																						
8B																						
8C																						
8D																						
8 (postcranial)	P	P	P	P		1	1		3	3		2		2	1					2	3	
10																			1			1
12A						1			1	1				1	1						1	
12B									1	1				1	1						1	

TABLE 68, cont.

Burial	Max	Mand	Ear		IOP	Humerus			Radius			Ulna			Hand			Scap		Clav		Ster
			L	*R*		*L*	*R*	*U*	*L*	*R*	*U*	*L*	*R*	*U*	*L*	*R*	*U*	*L*	*R*	*L*	*R*	
13A	1	1	1	1																		
13B	1		1	1			1										1	1			1	
13C	1	1	1	1	1			1														
13D	1	1																				
13 (mixed)						1	2															
14			J	J	J																	
15	1	1	1	1	1		1			1			1				1		1			
16A	1		1	1	1																	
16B																						
18A																						
18B																						
18C		1	1	1	1	1																
18D		1					1													1		
19A	J	J	J	J	J																	
19B								1														
20	1	1	1	1	1	1	1		1	1		1	1					1	1	1		
21A		1	1			1			1						1							
21B																1						
22A	1	1	1	1	1	1	1						1						1			
22B				1	1																	
22C	J	J																				
23	1	1	1	1	1	1			1	1		1	1					1				
24A	1	1				1	1							1				1				
24B	1	1																				
24C	1	1																				
24D	1	1																				
24 (mixed)			3	2	3	2			1		1		1					1	1			

TABLE 68, cont.

		Vert				*Inom*			*Femur*			*Pat*		*Tibia*			*Fibula*			*Foot*		
Burial	*Ribs*	*C*	*T*	*L*	*Sac*	*L*	*R*	*U*	*L*	*R*	*U*	*L*	*R*	*L*	*R*	*U*	*L*	*R*	*U*	*L*	*R*	*U*
13A			P			1	1		1	1				1	1							
13B						1	1		1	1		1	1	1	1				1	1	1	
13C									1	1				1	1				1			
13D																						
13 (mixed)												1		1	1					1	1	
14																						
15	P					1	1		1	1				1	1		1	1		1	1	
16A																						
16B										1				1							1	
18A							1		1	1				1	1							
18B						1	1		1	1				1	1					1	1	
18C									1		1			1	1		1	1		1	1	
18D	P		P	P					1	1				1	1		1	1			1	
19A																						
19B									1	1										1		
20	P		P			1	1		1	1			1	1	1		1	1				
21A	P	P	P	P		1			1											1		
21B	P	P	P	P	1	1	1				2					1						
22A									1	1				1	1				P	1	1	
22B																						
22C																						
23			P			1	1		1	1				1	1					1	1	
24A			P						1	1				1	1							
24B																						
24C																						
24D																						
24 (mixed)	P			P		1	3		2	1		2	1	2	2					1	1	

TABLE 68, cont.

Burial	Max	Mand	Ear L	Ear R	IOP	Humerus L	Humerus R	Humerus U	Radius L	Radius R	Radius U	Ulna L	Ulna R	Ulna U	Hand L	Hand R	Hand U	Scap L	Scap R	Clav L	Clav R	Ster
25A	1	1	1	1	1			1			1			1								
25B	J	J	J	J																		
26		1				1		1										1				
27	1	1	1	1	1	1	1		1			1			1							
28A	1	1																				
28 (mixed)	2	1		2		3	2				P			P					1		1	
29	J	J	J	J																		
30	1	1	1	1				1														
31A						1	1															
31B	J	J	J	J	J		J															
31C							1															
32						1	1															
33A	1	1	1	1	1	1	1				P	1	1					1	1			
33B	1	1	1	1	1	1	1		1	1		1	1					1		1		
33C	J	J	J	J	J																	
34	1	1		1		1				1	P					1						
35A	1	1	1	1		1	1		1	1		1	1				1					
35B	1	1	1	1		1	1							P				1		1	1	
35C	1	1								1												
35D																						
36A	1	1	1	1	1	1	1		1			1			1			1	1	1		
36B	1		1	1	1	1	1		1	1		1	1		1	1						
37A																			1			
37B	J	J	J	J	J																	
38A																						
38B																						
38C																						

TABLE 68, cont.

Burial	Ribs	Vert C	Vert T	Vert L	Sac	Inom L	Inom R	Inom U	Femur L	Femur R	Femur U	Pat L	Pat R	Tibia L	Tibia R	Tibia U	Fibula L	Fibula R	Fibula U	Foot L	Foot R	Foot U
25A						1	1		1	1				1	1					1		
25B																						
26			P	P	1	1	1		1	1						1		1				
27						1	1		1	1				1								
28A																						
28 (mixed)						1	1	P	1	3				3	2			1	P			
29		J	J																			
30									1	1				1	1				P	1		
31A			P			1	1			1	1			1	1				P	1		
31B									J	J				J	J		J	J				
31C						1	1		1	1												
32									1							1	1	1			1	
33A			P	P		1	1		1	1				1	1				P			1
33B						1	1		1	1		1		1	1				P		1	1
33C																						
34				P			1		1													
35A	P		P			1	1		1	1				1	1		1	1				
35B	P		P				1		1	1				1	1				P			
35C									1	1				1	1							
35D																						
36A	P		P	P		1	1		1	1		1	1	1	1					1	1	
36B	P		P			1	1		1	1				1	1		1	1		1	1	
37A									1	1				1	1							
37B																						
38A									J	J				J	J							
38B										1				1					P	1		
38C										1	1		1			1				1	1	

TABLE 68, cont.

Burial	Max	Mand	Ear		IOP	Humerus			Radius			Ulna			Hand			Scap		Clav		Ster
			L	R		L	R	U	L	R	U	L	R	U	L	R	U	L	R	L	R	
38D																						
38E	1	1	1	1	1																	
38 (mixed)	1,J	1,J		1										1								
40	1	1		1	1	1	1															
41A	J		J	J	J																	
41B	1										P											
44							1															
45															1							
46							1						1									
47	1	1	1	1	1																1	
48	1						1	1			1											
49		1	1		1	1	1					1				1			1			
51	1	1	1	1	1		1	1	1			1								1		
52A	J	J																				
52B		1																				
52C		1																				
52D	1	1																				
52 (mixed)			2	3	3	2	1					2	1	1					1			
53A	1		1	1																		
53B	1		1	1																		
53 (mixed)							1							1								
54	2		3	2	3																	
55A			J	J																		
55B	J	J	J	J	J																	
55C	1	1																				
55D	1	1																				

TABLE 68, cont.

		Vert				*Inom*			*Femur*			*Pat*		*Tibia*			*Fibula*			*Foot*		
Burial	*Ribs*	*C*	*T*	*L*	*Sac*	*L*	*R*	*U*	*L*	*R*	*U*	*L*	*R*	*L*	*R*	*U*	*L*	*R*	*U*	*L*	*R*	*U*
38D										J												
38E											1			1								
38 (mixed)									1													
40									1	1				1	1		1			1	1	
41A																						
41B									1	1						P			P			
44						1																
45									1	1												
46									1					1								
47		P	P			1			1	1		1				1				1	1	
48			P	P		1	1		1	1					1		1	1		1	1	
49						1	1		1	1												
51		P																				
52A											J											
52B																						
52C																						
52D																						
52 (mixed)						2	1		4	3	1			4	3				P			
53A																						
53B																						
53 (mixed)	P	P	P			1	1		2	2					1							
54									1													
55A																						
55B																						
55C																						
55D																						

TABLE 68, cont.

Burial	Max	Mand	Ear L	Ear R	IOP	Humerus L	Humerus R	Humerus U	Radius L	Radius R	Radius U	Ulna L	Ulna R	Ulna U	Hand L	Hand R	Hand U	Scap L	Scap R	Clav L	Clav R	Ster.
55 (mixed)			1	1	1	3	2	1,2J	1		P	1	2					1		1	1	
56	J		J																			
57	J	J	J																			
58		1			1		1															
59	J	J	J	J	J			J														
60	1	1	1	1	1																	
61A	1	1																				
61B		1																				
61C		1																				
61D		1																				
61E		1																				
61 (mixed)	2		3	2	2	4	5			3		4	1		1	1		3	1		2	
Stray fragments	1	1	1	1	2																	
Surface coll.	P	P											2				1					
Adult totals	52	55	45	45	41	37	41	9	11	14	6	17	18	6	6	5	5	14	12	10	8	0
Juvenile totals	13	14	15	13	9	0	1	4	0	0	0	0	0	0	0	0	0	0	0	0	0	0
"Present" totals	1	1	0	0	0	0	0	0	0	0	5	0	0	2	0	0	0	0	0	0	0	0

TABLE 68, cont.

Burial	Ribs	Vert C	Vert T	Vert L	Sac	Inom L	Inom R	Inom U	Femur L	Femur R	Femur U	Pat L	Pat R	Tibia L	Tibia R	Tibia U	Fibula L	Fibula R	Fibula U	Foot L	Foot R	Foot U
55 (mixed)	P	P	P	P		2	2		2	2	P	1	1	2	2			1	P		1	
56																						
57																						
58									1	1						1						
59											J											
60		P							1	1										1	1	
61A																						
61B																						
61C																						
61D																						
61E																						
61 (mixed)	P	P	P	P	2	5	3		5	7				3	2		1	2		2	1	
Stray fragments																				1		
Surface collection	P								1	1	P	1		2							1	
Adult totals	0	0	0	0	5	39	38	2	71	70	9	13	9	57	49	6	12	15	0	29	30	2
Juvenile totals	0	1	1	0	0	0	0	1	3	3	3	0	0	2	2	0	1	1	0	0	0	0
"Present" totals	17	9	21	13	0	0	0	1	0	0	2	0	0	0	0	1	0	0	17	0	0	0

Appendix E

TABULATION OF AGE, SEX, BURIAL FORM, BURIAL POSITION, ORIENTATION, AND NUMBER OF INDIVIDUALS PER BURIAL FOR THE TURNER SITE CEMETERY

Key

Columns 1 and 2 serve to designate each individual from each burial which was complete enough for analysis. Column 1 gives the burial number; column 2 gives the individual number. The individual numbers may be converted into the letters used in the text as follows: "1" becomes "A" in the case of multiple burials, but is ignored in the case of single burials; "2" becomes "B"; "3" becomes "C"; and so forth.

Column 3 gives the number of individuals in each burial.

In column 4, the variable Sinmul refers to whether a burial is single or multiple. A "1" means single, a "2" means multiple.

Column 5 is individual age. A "1" means under age 15, a "2" means over age 15, and a "0" means age is unknown.

Column 6 is sex. A "1" is a male, a "2" is a female, and a "0" is an individual of unknown sex.

Column 7 is burial form. A "1" means articulated, a "2" means partly articulated, a "3" means bundle, a "4" means single skull, and a "0" means form is unknown.

Column 8 is certainty of form. A "0" means form is completely uncertain, a "2" means form is probable, and a "1" means that form is definitely known.

Column 9 gives position for the articulated and partly articulated burials. A "1" means extended supine, a "2" means a position other than extended supine, and a "0" means that position is irrelevant because the burial is disarticulated.

Column 10 provides the orientation of the articulated and partly articulated burials. A "0" means the information is missing or irrelevant. The other numbers are explained below:

1 = N	5 = E	9 = S	13 = W
2 = NNE	6 = ESE	10 = SSW	14 = WNW
3 = NE	7 = SE	11 = SW	15 = NW
4 = ENE	8 = SSE	12 = WSW	16 = NNW

TABLE 69 Tabulation of Age, Sex, Burial Form, Burial Position, Orientation, and Number of Individuals per Burial for the Turner Site Cemetery

Burial	*Indiv*	*Persons In Burial*	*Sinmul*	*Age*	*Sex*	*Burial Form*	*Cert*	*Pos'n*	*Orient*
1	1	3	2	2	0	3	1	0	0
1	2	3	2	0	0	3	1	0	0
1	3	3	2	0	0	3	1	0	0
2	Femur 2	2	2	2	1	0	0	0	0
2	Femur 1	2	2	2	2	0	0	0	0
3	1	1	1	1	0	4	2	0	0
4	1	1	1	2	0	1	2	1	6
5	1	4	2	2	1	1	1	1	6
5	2	4	2	2	2	1	1	1	6
5	3	4	2	2	2	1	1	1	6
5	4	4	2	1	0	0	0	0	0
7	1	1	1	2	2	2	1	1	7
8	1	4	2	2	0	1	2	1	6
8	2	4	2	2	0	3	1	0	0
8	3	4	2	1	0	4	0	0	0
8	4	4	2	2	1	3	1	0	0
12	1	2	2	2	2	1	1	1	6
12	2	2	2	2	2	1	1	1	6
13	1	5	2	2	2	1	1	1	13
13	2	5	2	2	2	1	1	1	13
13	3	5	2	2	2	1	1	1	13
13	4	5	2	2	0	3	1	0	0
13	5	5	2	0	0	3	1	0	0
14	1	1	1	1	0	4	2	0	0
15	1	1	1	2	2	1	1	2	6
16	1	2	2	2	1	3	1	0	0
16	2	2	2	2	2	3	1	0	0
18	1	4	2	2	2	1	1	1	5
18	2	4	2	2	2	1	1	1	5
18	3	4	2	2	2	3	1	0	0
18	4	4	2	2	2	3	1	0	0
19	1	2	2	1	0	4	1	0	0
19	2	2	2	2	2	1	1	1	5
20	1	1	1	2	1	1	1	1	6
21	1	2	2	2	1	1	2	1	5
21	2	2	2	2	2	1	2	1	5
22	1	3	2	2	1	3	1	0	0
22	2	3	2	2	0	4	1	0	0
22	3	3	2	1	0	4	2	0	0
23	1	1	1	2	1	1	1	1	6
24	1	4	2	2	1	1	1	1	6
24	2	4	2	2	0	4	1	0	0
24	3	4	2	2	2	3	1	0	0

TABLE 69, cont.

Burial	Indiv	Persons In Burial	Sinmul	Age	Sex	Burial Form	Cert	Pos'n	Orient
24	4	4	2	2	2	3	1	0	0
25	1	2	2	2	2	1	1	1	6
25	2	2	2	1	0	1	1	1	6
26	1	1	1	2	1	1	1	1	6
27	1	1	1	2	2	1	1	1	6
28	1	3	2	2	2	1	1	1	6
28	2	3	2	2	2	3	1	0	0
28	3	3	2	2	2	3	1	0	0
29	1	1	1	1	0	1	1	1	7
30	1	1	1	2	2	1	1	1	13
31	1	3	2	2	2	1	1	1	6
31	2	3	2	1	0	1	1	1	6
31	3	3	2	2	1	1	1	1	6
32	1	1	1	2	2	1	1	2	6
33	1	3	2	2	1	1	1	1	6
33	2	3	2	2	1	1	1	1	6
33	3	3	2	1	0	4	1	0	0
34	1	1	1	2	2	1	1	1	15
35	1	4	2	2	2	1	1	1	6
35	2	4	2	2	2	1	1	1	6
35	3	4	2	2	2	1	1	1	6
35	4	4	2	1	0	4	2	0	0
36	1	2	2	2	1	1	1	1	6
36	2	2	2	2	2	1	1	1	6
37	1	2	2	1	0	4	2	0	0
37	2	2	2	2	2	1	1	1	6
38	1	5	2	1	0	1	2	1	6
38	2	5	2	2	2	1	2	1	6
38	3	5	2	2	1	1	2	1	6
38	4	5	2	1	0	1	2	1	6
38	5	5	2	2	2	1	2	1	6
39	1	1	1	1	0	4	2	0	0
40	1	1	1	2	2	1	1	1	6
41	1	2	2	1	0	4	2	0	0
41	2	2	2	2	2	3	2	0	0
43	1	1	1	2	0	1	2	1	5
44	1	1	1	2	0	1	2	1	14
45	1	1	1	2	2	1	1	1	6
46	1	1	1	2	1	1	2	1	14
47	1	1	1	2	2	1	1	1	13
48	1	1	1	2	2	1	2	1	6
49	1	1	1	2	2	1	2	1	14
51	1	1	1	2	1	1	1	1	6
52	1	5	2	1	0	0	0	0	0

TABLE 69, cont.

Burial	*Indiv*	*Persons In Burial*	*Sinmul*	*Age*	*Sex*	*Burial Form*	*Cert*	*Pos'n*	*Orient*
52	Femurs 2&7	5	2	2	2	1	2	1	6
52	Femur 3	5	2	2	2	0	0	0	0
52	Femurs 4&5	5	2	2	1	3	2	0	0
52	Femurs 1&6	5	2	2	1	0	0	0	0
53	1	2	2	2	2	3	1	0	0
53	2	2	2	2	2	3	1	0	0
55	1	5	2	1	0	4	2	0	0
55	2	5	2	1	0	4	1	0	0
55	3	5	2	2	1	1	2	1	6
55	4	5	2	2	1	0	0	0	0
55	Femur 3	5	2	2	2	0	0	0	0
56	1	1	1	1	0	1	1	1	7
57	1	1	1	1	0	4	2	0	0
59	1	1	1	1	0	1	1	1	5
60	1	1	1	2	1	1	1	1	14

www.ingramcontent.com/pod-product-compliance
Lightning Source LLC
LaVergne TN
LVHW050021250826
846302LV00008B/50